Beautifully Broken

A Journey Through the Bible for Parents of Children with Special Needs

Jen McIntosh

WESTBOW
PRESS®
A DIVISION OF THOMAS NELSON
& ZONDERVAN

WestBow Press books may be ordered through booksellers or by contacting:

WestBow Press
A Division of Thomas Nelson & Zondervan
1663 Liberty Drive
Bloomington, IN 47403
www.westbowpress.com
1 (866) 928-1240

ISBN: 978-1-9736-0406-8 (sc)
ISBN: 978-1-9736-0407-5 (e)

Library of Congress Control Number: 2017914267

Print information available on the last page.

WestBow Press rev. date: 02/07/2018

Contents

Preface

I am so glad you are reading this book! If you're here, you are most likely a parent or caregiver of a child with special needs. You may feel isolated, confused, desperate, and afraid. You may feel alone and abandoned. You may be worried and exhausted. Trust me, I have been there. Sometimes I still feel every one of those emotions. But one thing that has given me peace in the dark days is knowing that even though our children's special needs may be very different from one another, we're really all in this together. We can all relate to feeling like we don't belong, that no one gets the brokenness we feel inside, and that no one could understand our pain. Our journey has taken a major detour from the path we'd so blissfully been traveling. We've been dragged down into the ditch, slung through the mud, and have watched our dreams fade into the dust.

I understand what it's like to hold on to hope and assurances with every ounce of strength you've got, only to realize you'd hoped in the wrong thing and you'd counted on assurances that were never given. Boy, do I get it. What's most important is that our heavenly Father gets it. He understands how you feel. He is not taken by surprise that you are facing these painful issues. He knew this new normal awaited you. And He alone is our solid foundation for the trials we all will face. He is what we need. He is the One we live for. In God's promises, you can find assurance that He will come to your aid in whatever situation you may be facing with your precious child. He has your back on your new journey and is walking the path alongside you.

My son Liam is severely, multiply-disabled. He is a surviving micro-preemie twin; a term used to describe a very low birth weight baby. Only twenty-four weeks into my pregnancy, my boys were born unexpectedly. Each weighed only one pound and could fit in the palm of our hand. Brady died after a day and a half of fighting. Every time Liam had to be revived death's door sat waiting, welcome and open, hoping to usher him in as well. Against the odds Liam survived the danger only to see unfortunate statistics waiting next in line for their chance to have a go at him. They accumulated en masse and have torn his life apart. Liam cannot walk and cannot talk; in fact, he cannot take care of himself in any way at all. He is fully dependent on others to do everything for him. He relies on a wheelchair to get around but mostly enjoys life from his preferred position on the floor. Down there, his body doesn't have to work against his ever-present enemy: gravity. He has numerous diagnoses because of his very early start in life. His rare form of cerebral palsy is the most significant and impacting. Our family was thrown into utter chaos when he arrived, and it's taken years for us to reach any kind of normalcy. It is still completely off-kilter. Our life is not at all normal compared with how it used to be. Life was irreversibly and forever changed the day Liam was born. We were caught up in a whirlwind and thrown off our course. Little did we know just how far off our beaten path we would be taken.

God will lead us to scary, broken places, places of pain, with a love for us that is so deep our doe- eyed faces can't even begin to take it all in at first. We are a work in progress, broken in places we don't even realize, until we witness up close the brokenness in others.

In the years since Liam's birth, as we've grappled with significant challenges driving us to the foot of the cross, we have encountered God's abundant grace, ever flowing out to us even in the darkest of days. We have witnessed God showing up when we least expected Him but needed Him most. We have grown in far greater ways than we ever could have before Liam came along, and we have learned with a deeper understanding that although the plans we make can be devastatingly destroyed, beauty can arise from the ashes of the life we have left behind.

Everything has a purpose, including you, your child with special needs, and your individual journey. My prayer is that you will be able to draw nearer to God in the midst of your battles and will find a deep, abiding love for the Lord despite the pain and the darkness you face in your circumstances. I pray that this study will strengthen your trust in the One who created such a unique child as yours and that even though your life may be a thousand miles away from where it was, you will know God has your back and is holding your hand on your perfectly broken and bumpy road.

You are not alone.

Introduction

You may be wondering how you and your child could belong in a history book full of kings and queens, parting seas, and epic battles. You may be wondering if the Bible holds any wisdom at all for you and for the future you and your child with special needs face. Does God have anything to say about the brokenness, the suffering, the disabilities that now fill your day-to-day life? How can His Word even remotely relate to you with everything you have going on? After all, Jesus didn't have to care for a child with significant special needs.

Would it be surprising to know we actually can learn quite a lot about disabilities from the scriptures? Stories of suffering abound in both the Old and the New Testaments. The wise verse from Ecclesiastes 1:9 says "there is nothing new under the sun," and it's true. Lessons on pain, weakness, illness, and even disabling special needs can be found in God's Word. We will look into history and discover what God has to say about the brokenness we experience in our daily life of caring for children with special needs. Whether you are dealing with autism, ADHD, cerebral palsy, Down syndrome, a neurological disorder, or another genetic condition or special need, God has a plan for you and your child. He reveals to us through His Word just how very much He loves us. He loves the downtrodden, the despised, the destitute, and yes, even the disabled! Thank God that He speaks of sufferings in His Word so we are not left to flounder around without any guidance. The road He calls us down does not lead to a dead end!

Some statistics number Americans with disabilities at around one in six. When I cite that figure most people are quite shocked. Not everyone with a disability looks like they have a disability. People don't realize how many folks with hidden disabilities are sitting in the church pews right alongside them every Sunday morning. People assume disabilities impact people only physically, but the brokenness and suffering that take place internally are just as crippling. These disabilities are simply manifested differently. You are in good company if you or your loved ones experience a disability of some sort. Brokenness and disabilities are all around us.

In His earthly travels, Jesus engaged with people suffering many disabilities. He spoke with them, ministered to them, touched them, and would even heal them. He walked His talk. What society wanted nothing to do with and didn't desire, the very ones people shunned and viewed as the lowest of the low, Jesus esteemed and gave immense value. He had a deep, abiding love for hurting people. Jesus didn't blindly look the other way when He encountered the broken. He loved them and gave them hope. He gave them worth. He saw through their brokenness to the God-given beauty within.

My prayer for you as you go through this study is that you will feel complete freedom to engage in the mission God has called you to as a special needs parent. I pray this study will refresh your heart where it was once weary, giving you sincere joy entangled with peace that can be found only in journeying onward with Jesus.

Week 1
Why Me?

Out of suffering have emerged the strongest souls; the most massive characters are sealed with scars.

—Khalil Gibran

Introduction

As the parent of a child with special needs, you have probably asked God the typical questions people pose when things go wrong in their lives: "Where are You, God? Why me? How could this be happening to me? What did I do wrong? Am I not good enough? Why not someone who doesn't love You or who doesn't even think You exist? Why do I deserve this? Am I being punished? Is my child insignificant to You?" Others might not question God when they face a difficult situation. They are able to continue on with their lives, moving easily through trials and tribulations and accepting their unfortunate circumstances without question. They don't wonder and they don't despair. They figure that this is their lot in life, and they are able to adjust without much prayer or consideration of the situation. For them, it is what it is.

I have found myself camping out on both sides of the battlefield. I have been completely accepting of what was laid out before me. I didn't ask God any questions, and I didn't get mad; I just trudged through the nasty muck because that was the road I had been forced to take. I squared my shoulders, lifted my head high, and marched on, deciding that life was miserable and that I just needed to suck it up. Being a crybaby wouldn't get anything accomplished in the long run.

At some point, I broke emotionally. My strength and determination could take me only so far. I was missing something in my steady march to my own drumbeat. I realized my attitude was preventing me from seeking an authentic relationship with the conductor of my symphony, and I needed to get in tune with what He wanted from me.

I found myself continually asking God how He could have given such a unique and special child to me when He could have chosen any number of people who would have done a significantly better job. I didn't feel worthy of the honor or of the substantial responsibility I had been given. Why would God choose someone so unqualified for this job? Why would He allow my precious son—and ultimately our family—to suffer so severely? My questions returned to me echoing back out of the silence, but instead of "Why me?" I was startled to hear "Why not me?"

You might be in the first camp, repeatedly questioning God, needing answers, and seeking comfort in any response as you try to understand why this happened to you, your family, and your child. Some of us are born questioners, seeking answers to riddles and asking why at every turn. You might have a million questions but be too scared to speak them out loud. You may wonder if, as a faith-filled Christian, you should be asking any questions at all of the holy God who created your unique child. With our nurturing human spirit and our parental instincts, we naturally desire to try to understand why good people suffer and bad things happen.

God is not confused about the circumstances you face. He didn't wake up surprised to see you now have a child with special needs. He knows exactly where you are. He even knows what you are thinking. He hears the cries of your heart. He is wholly with you in your struggles, and He sees your heartache.

Sweet friends, as we dive into the Word this week, let us pray that God will allow us to gain a deeper trust of Him through our trials. His Word gives us promises for our pain, for the longing in our hearts, and for the aches deep down in our souls. He is trustworthy. He hears our cries of "Why me?" and He wants to take us by the hand and to draw us near.

> "For I am the Lord your God who takes hold of your right hand and says to you, Do not fear; I will help you" (Isa. 41:13).

The Bible isn't full of perfect people with polished plans. Alleluia! It's full of real people with messy lives who are suffering hardships with hurts down deep in their hearts. We witness people who are enduring brokenness and are in need of breakthroughs. Some of them pray, crying out to God, seeking to know why. Let's take a look at Job—a decent, upright guy who was forced to face unimaginable suffering. Let's see what the Lord has to say when Job questions him.

Read Job 1.

Who was Job?_____

_____

_____

What does the Bible mean when it refers to Job as being upright?_____

_____

_____

What did Job do that shows his respect and submission to God? _____

_____

Job was a man who had much to be thankful for. He had everything he ever needed. He was a great and godly man, even going so far as to make sacrifices on behalf of his children in case they had sinned against God. He was well-known and well-liked. He had status in his community. Nothing bad could be said about him. His large holdings of livestock testified to his wealth. He was blessed with a wife, servants, good health, and numerous children. He was living an amazing life full of abundance. By all accounts, Job had everything going for him. But Satan was lurking behind the scenes and wanted to take everything from him. Satan planned to do what he does best: cause turmoil, chaos, and pain. Satan wanted to yank Job right out of his safe, comfortable world.

Satan desired deception. He wanted a chance to disprove God's confidence in Job. Satan scoffed at and mocked God, telling Him Job had no reason to complain, because God had protected him from all imaginable harm. What could there possibly be for Job to criticize God about when he had gotten everything in life he might desire?

Here in Job 1 we get a glimpse of the spiritual battles that take place unseen by human eyes. What we perceive or think is happening is not what is actually going on behind the scenes.

With God's approval, Job would experience the loss of everything he held dear. He could do nothing as he watched all of his life's achievements come to a devastating end. Life as he knew it would be over. Job would have everything ripped away for reasons unknown to him.

What do you notice about Satan's abilities? _____

_____

How did Job initially react when the night came to a close? _____

_____

Read Job 1:21.
"May the name of the Lord _____."

Job praised God from the beginning. Job recognized God for who He is: sovereign and omnipotent. The Lord gives and the Lord can take away, and in humility Job fully acknowledged the authority of God. Most of us would scream about the unfairness of a night like the one Job suffered, but Job did just the opposite. Instead of yielding to despondency and hopelessness, he remained calm and accepted his fate. Job praised God, knowing it was He who gave him the privilege of so many blessings to enjoy in the first place.

Read Job 1:22.
"In all this, Job_____ by charging_____ with _____."

In the NIV translation, at first glance, we read that Job didn't charge God with wrongdoing, which sounds like he didn't make accusations against God, blaming Him for the day's disasters. This translation seems a bit out of character given what we already know of Job. This verse can be better understood in the original translation of "charged with wrongdoing" from the Hebrew, "nor vented forth against God." A more nuanced translation for English readers would be "nor yelled foolishly against God." That makes more sense when we look at Job's personality. Remember, God had pointed Job out as an upright man. This verse speaks highly of Job, saying that in all the sufferings he had experienced thus far, Job had not sinned by holding God responsible for it. Job did not bear any ill will or anger toward God for the tragedies that had befallen him. He didn't rail against God and make false accusations. Job was still an upright and blameless guy, humble before the Lord.

Why do you think Job was able to be so accepting of his horrible circumstances?_____

_____

_____

What comparison does Job make with a newborn baby? _____

_____

How does this relate to the losses he has experienced? _____

_____

Read Job 2:3–10.

God had proven Satan wrong in his futile attempts to prove God wrong. God was not obliged to prove him wrong. He owed Satan no such privilege, but God knew Job would remain a good man no matter what Satan attempted to do to him.

Satan was the one sorely disappointed when his initial attempts to ruin Job didn't succeed. Satan took everything from him and he didn't get the response from Job he expected. God was vindicated in discrediting Satan. As his pride took a hit, Satan's frustration mounted. He was sure he could still prove to God that Job wasn't worthy of God's favor and affection.

Satan's assumption that Job would despair of his circumstances and curse God for all of the troubles that had befallen him was so far off the mark that he quickly devised another plan to try to prove God wrong. Satan wanted just one more opportunity with Job to prove God didn't have a faithful, righteous man in him. He wanted one more shot at trying to prove God was a liar, just like he had tried to do with Eve in the garden of Eden. Satan desired to weaken Job's mind and heart in order to turn him from God.

What is the one thing God will not allow Satan to do? _____
_____

When Satan accused Job of valuing his health above all else, God allowed Satan to deliver one final, excruciatingly painful blow. With Job's integrity on the line, Satan afflicted him with a serious medical condition. Job's good health was allowed to be taken from him.

What affliction did Job suffer from? _____

Job was cursed with a horribly disfiguring disease. He suffered from painful sores from the soles of his feet to the top of his head. They would blister, scab over, and turn black. We cannot be certain what the exact ailment Job suffered from, but the Hebrew word for it was *shechiyn*, which is singular in origin and means "burning sore." Because Job was stricken from his head to his toes, we can assume that his body was literally one giant, burning sore. We can't even begin to imagine the pain he would have been in.

The effects of Job's illness were plentiful and devastating. Job was miserable. In his time, this was a hopeless, painful disease with no promise of relief. No doctor and no medicine could keep the disease at bay. The deaths of Job's children had finality. He could eventually heal from such a heavy blow and move on. But this disease brought him pain without an end.

List some of the effects of Job's disease.

1) _____ (v. 2:8)
2) _____ (v. 2:12)
3) _____ (v. 7:5)
4) _____ (v. 7:14)
5) _____ (v. 16:8)
6) _____ (v. 19:17)
7) _____ (v. 19:20)
8) _____ (v. 30:17)
9) _____ (v. 30:30)

How did Job's wife respond to his condition? (v. 2:9) _____
_____

How did Job answer her? (v. 2:10) _____
_____

Job's disturbed wife wasn't as kind and generous as her husband in regards to her language. She had experienced heavy losses as well, losing her children and her wealth too. She was hurt and angry. She tried to get Job to curse God for all the troubles he had endured. She believed Job would be better off dead than facing a lifetime with his horrible health condition. And we see this today, don't we? We hear doctors, the educated, and society say life isn't worth living if a person faces a bleak prognosis, as if our abilities somehow determine our worth. We see a disability diagnosis in the womb leading to calls for abortion from misguided doctors warning of difficult issues. Women terminate a pregnancy under the guise of being humane instead of letting God have the final say. We even see adults seek out euthanasia in order to exempt themselves from the hardships that will come with their painful diagnosis. In all this, we are told that ending a life is the kind, even moral, thing to do. A life full of pain, hardships, and unknowns, is believed by some to be better off not living.

But Job refused to take part in his wife's idea of solace. Despite losing his health, Job acknowledged God's sovereignty and His right to bring bad as well as good things into our lives. Job asked his wife a fundamental question still asked today: do we accept only good from God and never bad? Job refused to abandon his faith just because he didn't understand his circumstances.

Job did not turn away from God with his question. He was matter of fact and realistic. But he did start to despair of his current situation with complaints, appeals, and inquiries. Job starts to wrestle with his lot in life and the weight of what he has to bear.

Read Job 3.

What did Job curse and why did he do this?_____

_____

Job cursed the day he was born. He felt it would have been better if he had never been born at all. He would never have had to experience the loss of his children if he could have just been born dead. He wouldn't have faced disease and money problems. Job couldn't see any purpose to his suffering. He thought his life was meaningless and wondered why he existed. To Job, everything is meaningless. He feels his life is pointless. If he had never existed, neither would any of the horrible tragedies or his failing health. He had faced unimaginable pain and loss and could not understand why this had to happen to him. He was suffering and for what reason? Job was, after all, a good man, and bad things weren't supposed to happen to good people, right?

How many times do you read the word *why* in this chapter?_____

Job bemoaned his very existence, finding no purpose in his circumstances; he was despondent and without hope. This leads Job to now question God over and over. Job wants to understand. What is his purpose? Why did God let him be born since life had brought him so much suffering?

Read Job 7:2–10.

How long did Job's suffering continue?_____

_____

What did Job see as his only escape?

_____

Read Job 7:11.

"Therefore I will not keep silent: I will _____ in the anguish of my spirit, I will _____ in the bitterness of my soul."

What did Job say he was going to do?_____

_____

Read Job 9:14–16.

"How can I _____ with him? How can I find words to _____ with him? Though I were innocent, I could not answer him; I could only plead with my judge for mercy. Even if I summoned him and he responded, I do not believe he would give me a hearing."

Read Job 19:7.

"Though I cry _____ I get no response; though I call for help, there is no justice."

Job now questioned his situation with greater intensity and despair out of the longings of his heart. He cried out for justice for all of the wrongs committed against him. He spoke out through his anguish, complaining about what he had to endure. Job knew God could see him and was mindful of his sufferings. Job was in full on gripe mode and he wanted to have his voice heard. He wanted to have his day in court so his testimony could be heard.

He wanted to have an audience with God.

Read Job 19:13–19.

Who had abandoned Job? _____

Job was bitter and angry. Everyone had left him. He didn't deserve what he was forced to endure. He could not comprehend any cause for the trials he faced. He saw no reason that he should suffer so. Job was comfortless and losing all hope. None of it made sense, and Job wanted to understand what he had done to bring about such severe judgments from God.

I think most of us special needs parents can relate to the impassioned reaction of Job. We see our children forced to endure such difficult issues such as health problems, physical impairments, emotional issues, language difficulties, and learning disabilities, and we believe it isn't fair that they have to go through such trials. We watch our children suffer in multiple ways that typical families will never experience. We even ask why on our own behalf. We whine and complain about what we have to deal with every day—doctor visits, therapy appointments, phone calls, paperwork, insurance issues, school problems, IEP's—and we can get angry at the inequality of it all. We can't understand why life has to be like this for us and our families. It doesn't make sense. This was never in our plans. We feel it is unfair that our children have to live such difficult and sometimes painful lives, and we ask God why, just like Job did.

Have you ever felt that your child's special needs are unfair?_____

_____

_____

Have you ever compared your child's special needs to another child's, thankful your child's aren't worse?_____

_____

Listen to Job's complaining:

"Does it please you to oppress me, to spurn the work of your hands, while you smile on the schemes of the wicked?" (Job 10:3).

"Then know that God has wronged me and drawn his net around me. Though I cry, 'I've been wronged!' I get no response; though I call for help, there is no justice" (Job 19:6–7).

"As surely as God lives, who has denied me justice, the Almighty, who has made me taste bitterness of soul" (Job 27:1).

"He [God] throws me into the mud, and I am reduced to dust and ashes. I cry out to you, O God, but you do not answer; I stand up, but you merely look at me" (Job 30:19–20).

"Oh, that I had someone to hear me! I sign now my defense—let the Almighty answer me; let my accuser put his indictment in writing" (Job 31:35).

What adjectives come to mind when you read Job's feelings?_____
_____

Have you accused God of not caring about your situation with your special needs child? _____
_____

Have you wondered how the suffering you experience could accomplish anything? _____
_____

Insert your name in all the "me" spots in Job's sentences, and you'll likely realize you've used similar language on occasion. You might not sound as poetic and elegant as Job, but the gist is exactly the same: you desire a reason for your child's sufferings and your own. We wrestle with the "why" questions more often than we might even realize.

Job showed he has attitude in these verses. He was angry and determined to questioned the morality of the judgments made against him. He felt he'd been wronged, it was unfair, and he couldn't make sense of it. Job was sure God must have been angry at him. He wanted to know what was being accomplished from all he was enduring.

Do you think it is sinful to get angry with God?_____

_____

Have you been angry at God?_____

_____

Have you felt like He doesn't care?_____

_____

Have you tried to get God to explain why you face the circumstances you do with your special needs child? _____

_____

Read Job 23:3-4, 8-12.

Never doubting God's existence and sovereignty, Job just wanted to understand. Even though Job could not see God, he trusted God was involved behind the scenes. Job would boldly go to God's residence to make his case known and hear what He would say if Job only knew where it was. Job had always treasured God's words, following after Him throughout his life. Even when Job couldn't see God he was confident God could see him.

Finally, among all of Job's frustrations and from a raging thunderstorm, Job finally got the audience with God he'd so desperately wanted and demanded.

Read Job 38 and 39.

"Where were you when _____?" (v. 38:4).

"Who marked off its _____?" (v. 38:5).

"Have you ever given _____ to the morning, or shown dawn its _____?" (v. 38:12).

How did God answer Job?_____

_____

_____

In chapters 38 and 39, God had a list of criticisms for Job. God asked question after question about what Job could do or what knowledge Job truly had about reality. Remember how many times Job asked "Why?" in chapter 3, and compare that to how many questions God had for Job in return.

God's questioning continued on through chapters 40 and 41. He posed these queries to Job not to exalt Himself, not to show off, but to teach Job just how little he actually understood about divine creation. God showed His omniscience. He reminded Job about the beauty of creation and about the wonders of His works. He reminded Job that He alone was God, and He explained some of the workings of the world that Job had not comprehended. God even described His creation to him—from the light to the dark, from lions to lambs, from donkeys to eagles. God opened Job's eyes, giving him a brand new perspective he'd never seen before, directly from the One who created it all.

After reading these two chapters, you might find it very frustrating that God didn't even answer Job's specific questions. God took the time to meet with Job but didn't give him what he so desperately wanted: a reason for his sufferings. God reached down into Job's heart, enveloping him in a reality he had never before considered. God made Job step outside of himself in order to illustrate that there was a much bigger picture. He gave Job an opportunity to visualize a world outside of man's small, self-centered thinking, by illuminating one that is spiritual, with a breadth and a depth that surpass all human imagining.

Read Job 40:2.

"Will the one who _____ with the Almighty _____ him? Let him who _____ God _____ him!"

God put Job on the stand and asked if Job had the audacity to correct Him.

God was trying to show Job that the world He created has an order that we may not understand because we can't fully perceive it. We get only a tiny glimpse of the workings of God. We human beings are unable to fully comprehend the mind of God, the working out of things unseen to fulfill His will. In 1 Corinthians 13:12 Paul says, "Now we see but a poor reflection as in a mirror; then we shall see face to face. Now I know in part; then I shall know fully, even as I am fully known." Paul is saying our vision is blurry, like looking through smudged glasses. People in his time didn't have the shiny, silvered mirrors we have today, allowing us to see our reflections in fine detail. They had dark, brassy mirrors that only offered very poor reflections. Paul recognized that our awareness of our world is imperfect. We don't get a crystal-clear image but are afforded only a dark, fuzzy view for now.

All of us believers will face the same struggle as Job, trying to make sense of things we can't fully see or grasp with our finite minds. This seeker mindset is obviously not limited to us special needs parents. Like Job, we seek answers, hoping to get them when we try to make sense of our situations. We wrestle with why and hope for an answer.

Read Job 19:25–27.

"I know that my _____ lives and that in the _____ He will stand upon the _____. And after my skin has been destroyed, yet _____ I will _____: I myself will see him with _____."

What is Job certain of? _____

Is it comforting to know God has a purpose you might not be able to see or understand?_____

_____

_____

Read Job 40:4.

"I am _____ how can I reply to you?"

Read Job 42:1–6.

Here in chapter 42 we see Job finally say to God, "I get it." He understood there was deeper and more meaningful purpose to life's circumstances than what he gets the opportunity to experience and know. God can never be measured against our human standard of judgment. Job humbly acknowledged that his perception was unquestionably limited and that God's plan was ultimately supreme. Job was impressed that the God of all creation would even offer him an audience after all of his whining and questioning.

In the end, Job did not get the response he initially sought. He didn't get a pleasing answer for why he had to suffer such terrible trials and afflictions, but he fully understood that they were all a part of God's greater plan. Job walked away from his audience with the Lord knowing that ultimately, the trials he faced and his earthly afflictions would pale in comparison with the glory of one day being face to face with the majesty and grandeur of the sovereign, creator God. Job started out asking "Why me?" and ended up with no definitive answer. God told Job, "It's not your right to understand everything. I don't owe you an explanation. Trust that I am running things behind the scenes and you are not in control."

Knowing God sees the whole picture, do you feel you can put greater trust in Him?_____

_____

_____

What part of your own experience with asking God "Why?" comes to mind when you read Job's story?_____

_____

Read Job 42:7–16.

God did not view Job's anger as sinful. In fact, God doubly blessed Job in the end. Ultimately God reprimanded Job's friends for their know it all attitudes and for having attempted to incite and to agitate Job. Job's friends peppered their language with falsehoods about God and their self righteous attitudes about Job's problems made Job despair.

Read Job 42:7.

"After the Lord had said these things to Job, he said to Eliphaz the Temanite, 'I am _____ with you and your two friends, because _____ as my servant Job has.'"

In verses 7–8, God uses one adjective four times to describe Job. What is it? _____

What was the difference between Job and his friends that God got mad at them but not at Job?

_____

_____

Does this change your view on whether we are allowed to be angry with God?

_____

_____

Sometimes the ways in which God works in our lives is hard to fathom. Sometimes we forget that God is omniscient; He knows everything. That means He even knows how we feel. We tend to forget that. We forget that an omniscient God will know we are angry with Him even if we do not speak our thoughts aloud. There is no reason to hide from Him what we are thinking and feeling. Anger is a natural, appropriate, human emotion. God created us in His image and gave us this emotion for a reason. The problem lies in how we express our anger. This anger can draw us away from God creating a bitter divide between us, or it can propel us to the foot of His throne, leading us to seek an audience as Job did. If we face uncertainty, confusion, and pain, and our anger drives us to seek God's counsel and to know Him better, He will not see this anger as sinful.

Read Psalm 13.

Is David complaining to God?_____

_____

How does David feel at the beginning of this psalm?_____

_____

How does David end this psalm?_____

_____

Even the mighty King David, whose living epitaph is known as "a man after God's own heart," felt God was neglecting him. In his pain, David was real with his feelings and questioned God. But David balanced out his despair with hope. David never turned from God; he turned toward Him with passionate appeals.

The same can be said of Job. Everything Job went through in his sufferings would bring the best of us low. Despair, doubt, fear, and anger would be normal feelings at the loss of everything we hold dear. Yet through it all, we can have hope in God as Job did. Even amid our hardships, with uncertainty looming in our lives, we can trust that God knows what He is doing and is in full control. We can't clearly see the big picture yet.

Job's suffering shows us there could be times in our lives when we face trials and never know why God has allowed them to happen. Certainly, sin in our life can cause us to go through unnecessary pain, but at times our suffering will have no logical explanation that we can see. It will just happen. We aren't guaranteed an explanation. That doesn't mean we won't have pain and frustration in our circumstances and that we won't try to find some reasoning or understanding to make sense of it all. However, God is omnipresent and actively involved in our lives even when it doesn't seem like it; we are looking through smudged glasses! Asking God why is not a problem. Our challenge is to turn to him in spite of the why.

Read Ecclesiastes 11:5.

"As you do not know the path of the wind or how the body is formed in a mother's womb, so you cannot understand the work of God, the Maker of all things."

Group questions

Have you ever questioned God concerning your child's needs and asked, "Why me?"_____

_____

_____

Do you feel God owes you an explanation?_____

_____

Do you think you would be better equipped to handle your child's diagnosis if God gave you specific answers to your "Why's?"? _____

Does it scare you to realize life is out of your ability to control?_____

_____

Week 1 notes

_____
_____
_____
_____
_____
_____
_____
_____
_____

Jen's Journal
February 11

Nothing makes me feel more deficient in my God-given role as a mom than parenting a child with significant disabilities. I wake up every day and feel ill equipped to do this job. Why me? I wake up and a battle rages in my mind. Lines are drawn. One side is warring that I cannot possibly manage to do this job in any way that won't render my child broken and incapable; the other side warring that God chose Liam for me and that He evidently thinks I won't screw this up too badly.

You've probably heard this phrase: "God will never give me more than I can handle. I just wish He didn't trust me so much." I hate this phrase. I really do. It has gotten so overused and abused by people trying to comfort those who are going through tough times.

God does give us more than we can handle. All the time. It's no accident that He pushes us beyond the limits of what we think we are capable of handling. The apostle Paul was put through numerous situations that would make the best of us wither and give up. Paul boasted of how weak he was while suffering beatings, stonings, robberies, and shipwrecks. And all the while, God gave him more than a human could handle, lifting him up with His mercy and grace. (Oxymoronic if you aren't a Christian, I know.)

I just can't think of God in the way He comes across in that familiar phrase. He has His purposes. I know I wouldn't want God to give me a badge that says, "You've buried two children and didn't go crazy, so I guess I can trust you now!"

Could you imagine that kind of pressure? It's enough to kill you! God gives us a lot to deal with at times, and some of it is ugly. Really ugly. But He promises never to leave us when we are facing the ugly stuff.

The Bible tells us we are to rely on God to give us strength. We are to let Him carry our burdens. We are not to handle them all ourselves; we aren't meant to. Each day I wake up, warring within myself asking, "Why me?" and then I give everything to God because I trust He will equip me. One day at a time.

For I am the Lord,
your God, who takes hold
of your right hand & says
to you. Do not fear:
I will help you.

≫• Isaiah 41:13 •≪

Week 2
God's Providence and Sovereignty

The providence of God is like Hebrew words; it can be read only backwards.
—John Flavel

Introduction

Providence is not a commonly used word in Christian vernacular today. It seems to scare people off. Maybe we haven't understood providence in a way that we can articulate properly. Maybe when arguments arise about suffering and the goodness of God, we fall short as Christians in explaining our conclusion that one does not exclude the other. Are we scared to explain to a world that seeks perfection that disabilities are a part of God's plan and that those who are seen as "less than" were created with purpose and on purpose? Are we scared to admit that suffering does indeed bring God glory?

Providence is a significant and crucial aspect of God's character that we must try to fully understand to help us cope and to comprehend life's difficulties. The trials of a special needs family are not short lived, and will most likely be something you will have to endure for life. If we can gain a critical awareness of God's orchestration of life—the processes and natural means through which He accomplishes His will— we will be better able to survive the adversities that come our way. This will give us peace of mind and stability when we can't make sense of our circumstances.

God's providence goes hand in hand and overlaps with His sovereignty. While separate aspects of God, they both hold sway in our lives in ways we don't immediately recognize. We will look at both of these aspects of His character this week in order to help us see beyond ourselves to a God who is bigger than our circumstances. God is greater and wiser than we can possibly comprehend. He's in control for a reason.

Sweet friends, as we dive into scripture this week, let us pray that God will open our eyes to His wisdom, reveal to us His mighty hand in our lives, and allow us to see better the path on which He has chosen to lead us.

"Come, see a man who told me everything I ever did" (John 4:29).

First, let's define what *providence* means. According to *Merriam-Webster*, it is "divine guidance or care; God-conceived power guiding and sustaining human destiny."

The word *providence* is derived from the Latin *pro*, meaning "before," and *video*, meaning "to see."

In theological terms, providence means God, with His foresight, brings all things to pass, both seen and unseen. God's influence is not only over all of history; it is in all of history. As John Calvin explains, "God is the keeper of the keys. He governs all events."

Read Proverbs 16:9.
"The human mind plans the way, but the Lord _____ the steps."

Read Matthew 6:8.
"Do not be like them, for your Father _____ before you ask him."

Read Luke 1:52.
"He has _____ rulers from their thrones but has lifted up the humble."

Read Galatians 1:15–16.
"But when God, who _____ from birth and called me by his grace, was pleased to reveal his Son in me so that I might preach him among the Gentiles, I did not consult any man."

Do you see evidence for God's providence in these verses? _____
_____

Who allows rulers to be put on their thrones?_____

Read 1 Samuel 16:1.
"The Lord said to Samuel, 'How long will you mourn for Saul, since I have _____ him as king over Israel? Fill your horn with oil and be on your way; I am sending you to Jesse of Bethlehem. I have _____ one of his sons to be king.'"

What do you hear God saying in this verse? _____

_____

_____

Do you think God is showing favoritism here?_____

_____

_____

God has His reasons for choosing certain people for positions of authority and kingship. Many Christians have a healthy skepticism on why God would pick people whom they see as unworthy to be in position of leadership. (Look at any recent election, and you'll find Christians standing firmly on each side of the contest.) But does the success of the less likely candidate mean God has not providentially appointed them? Can God not work through appointed leaders to bring about His plan? Surely, He allows us dominion and free rein to make mistakes in picking leaders, politicians, and even presidents, in order to teach us, allowing us to learn through them as we go.

Read Genesis 50:20.
"You intended to _____, but God intended it for _____ to _____."
"What is now being done, the _____ of many _____."

If you are not familiar with the history of Joseph in Genesis, I highly encourage you to read deeper into chapters 37 to 50 this week. This won't take you long, and it will be worth your time. It's important to see how much evidence of God's providence is tucked into Joseph's history. The years leading up to Joseph's position of authority under Pharaoh had been full of family dysfunction, sibling rivalry gone wrong, abandonment, wrongful accusations of rape, and imprisonment. Joseph repeatedly suffered through unfortunate circumstances that seemed inexplicable and completely unfair. Joseph didn't deserve the bad things that happened to him, but he was fully confident that God's providence had led him through the situations he was forced to endure.

Joseph trusted God and knew He had used his thirteen years of slavery and imprisonment for a greater good. His ill fated circumstances had brought him to a position second only to Pharaoh. Who could have foreseen years earlier that a boy abandoned in a well, an accused attempted rapist, a forgotten prisoner, would eventually rise to a position of authority and would have the privilege of saving many people? Joseph was the last born son of a Hebrew family, the last person ever expected to rise to power in Egypt. No one could have seen that coming except God. He knew each negative turn of events were needed to eventually bring Joseph to a place of power and prestige to help save lives.

Read Genesis 50:21

"So then, don't be afraid. I will _____ for _____ and your _____." And he reassured them and spoke _____ to them.

Was Joseph bitter over his brothers' actions?_____

_____

Why not?_____

_____

Why do you think Joseph had such confidence in God's providence? _____

_____

Read Joshua 24:1–13.

Where did God lead Abraham? _____

Who gave Isaac to Abraham, and who gave Jacob and Esau to Isaac? _____

Who assigned land to Jacob and Esau? _____

Who sent Moses and Aaron to Egypt? _____

Who afflicted the Egyptians? _____

Who brought the Israelites out of Egypt? _____

What did God do to the pursuing Egyptians? _____

Who destroyed the Amorites and gave their land to the Israelites? _____

Whom did God use to bless His people? _____

Who gave the Israelites land for which they didn't toil? _____

In this passage we read about all of these different events that God brought to pass over a long period of time. Speaking through Joshua, God recites a brief history to the people reminding them of what He had done. God had previously promised Abraham that his seed, his family line, would inherit land that became known as the Promised Land (Gen. 12:7). This promise had been given to Abraham while he was still childless. The fulfillment of this promise took more than seven hundred years to come to fruition. Imagine that! Seven hundred years of God orchestrating events from natural disasters, the positioning of leaders, miracles of nature, and victories in war to bring the Israelites, Abraham's descendants, into position to finally gain the land faithfully promised to Abraham so many centuries before. God declared He had done all these things to position the people to claim the land. God always keeps his promises. The length and breadth of His providence knows no bounds! No detail is too small, or situation too big, and no length of time is too long to prevent God from accomplishing His will.

Read Ephesians 1:11–12.

"In _____ we were also chosen, having been _____ according to the plan of him who works out _____ in conformity with the _____ of His _____ in order that we, who were the first to _____ in _____, might be for the praise of his glory."

What does God work out? _____

What does God's purpose conform to? _____

We can see that every event occurs according to God's will. Paul is speaking of God's providence in running His creation. This passage emphasizes that God's will, not ours, takes place for His reasons alone.

People seem to have a hard time believing in God's providence when they see so many things that do not make sense. Pain, suffering, and evil make some people jump to the conclusion that God isn't good because He doesn't stop these things from happening. Thinking back to what we learned last week in Job, we have seen that God knew exactly what was going to happen to Job, allowed it to occur, and didn't intervene to prevent it. That seems like a tough pill to swallow. We might have difficulty wrapping our brains around that when we view Job's story according to the way we think it should have turned out. But we saw beautiful things emerge from the tragedies Job experienced. What did God say to Job? God told Job that his view was extremely limited. God had a greater plan working it's way out, unseen by human eyes. We don't get to see the ending. We don't get to write the final chapter. We don't get to see who is influenced by our experiences. We don't get to see how far our story ripples out and whom it will affect. We don't get the advantage of being omniscient and can't always know fully why things happen the way they do and for what purpose. What the world struggles and groans against, God shines His light brightly through. He delights in making beautiful endings out of messy beginnings.

Read Romans 8:28.

"And we know in all things God works for the _____ of those who love him and have been _____ according to His _____."

For whose good is God working? _____

What things work for God's good?_____

For whose purpose are things working? _____

This meaningful, oft-quoted verse gets misused a lot. First, Paul does not say this promise applies to everyone. He confines the working of good things to the people God has called, His people. This applies only to those of us who have put our hope and faith in Jesus Christ. Second, this verse doesn't say all things are good. We know this simply isn't true. Not all things in this fallen world are good.

God does not see rape as good.

God does not see racism as good.

God does not see murder as good.

God does not see adultery as good.

God does not see neglect of the poor as good.

We can tick off a long list of things that we know are not inherently good and that God absolutely opposes. God hates sin because He is holy and our sins separate us from Him. We see a lot of unexplained evil, but this has never been nor ever will be God's desire for His people. Many people mistakenly assume that when evil things happen it's because they are God's will. But we humans have the ability to make sinful choices resulting in terrible outcomes. It's the free will clause in our DNA. We want what we want despite the ramifications, and when we choose wrong, God lets us see what that looks like. He gives us what we want, and then we have the audacity to complain about the consequences.

What Paul is saying is that we can trust God in His providence to use a situation and funnel it toward our ultimate good, because all things work for the good. Work is an action. It's a process. It is effort used to accomplish a goal. Our circumstances need not always be perfect for everything to work out in the long run. We don't have to have our lives completely together for God to work things out for our betterment. Our infinite God can take the painful messes and the unpleasant realities of life and use them for a greater good. Our life is always a work in progress. He can change our perspective from one of woe to wow when we trust Him in the process.

When Paul wrote this message to the Romans he was going through difficult trials himself. Paul faced what seemed insurmountable troubles during his lifetime and he had a depth of experiences from which to write from:

- beaten with rods
- received 40 lashes minus one several times
- multiple imprisonments
- stoned
- stranded at sea
- shipwrecked three times
- severely persecuted

Paul didn't have an optimistic outlook because his life had been easy by any means. Paul's life was very hard! He was no stranger to suffering through various hardships. As special needs parents, we can relate to Paul's perspective; when things don't work out the way we thought they would, we can still witness good come from the setbacks.

Paul had a deep, abiding trust in the workings of God, believing that even when circumstances don't make sense, God has the situation firmly in his grasp. Paul trusted that we could relinquish our plans, because God has the blueprints. Paul fully relied on God's providence to bring greater good out of his situations. He works even in our difficulties to bring good things out of the bad.

Read 2 Corinthians 6:10.
"Sorrowful, yet always_____; poor, yet making many rich; having _____, and yet possessing _____."

What was Paul feeling here?_____
_____

How was his attitude? _____
_____
_____

Paul wrote this when he was old, poor, deserted, imprisoned, and in danger of immediate death. He didn't fight his circumstances but remained hopeful; despite the difficult situations he encountered, Paul remained committed to God and to God's purpose for his life. Paul didn't let his immediate position determine his ultimate perspective.

Reread Romans 8:28. What exactly does Paul mean by the good? _____
_____

Read Romans 8:29.
"For those God foreknew He predestined to be _____ to the _____
of His _____ that he might be the firstborn among many brothers."

This verse says that through our sufferings we are made more like Jesus. God works in our weaknesses, our struggles, our trials, and our brokenness to help our character; to mold us and shape our lives into the likeness of His son. Our good can be found only in Jesus Christ. As God works through us, our stories ultimately reveal His glory.

God's providence is all-powerful. He orchestrates what may seem to be trivial or insignificant details to achieve something beyond what we could imagine for our life. Sometimes we can look back and see a vast number of circumstances arranged to accomplish one purpose. What we may originally have considered mere coincidence will clearly reflect God's direct involvement in our lives. No plan of His can be thwarted. No detail is too small for Him. Remember: God is working things out even in the mundane events of our day-to-day lives. If things don't make sense just yet, that's okay. It doesn't have to make sense right now for everything to still be going according to God's plan.

Read John 5:3–17.
"Then Jesus said to him, 'Get up! Pick up your mat and walk.' At once the man was cured; he picked up his mat and walked" (vv. 8–9).

"Jesus said to them, 'My Father is always at his work to this very day, and I, too, am working'" (v. 17).

Who is always working?_____

Jesus had just performed an unbelievable miracle. He had given a physically disabled man the ability to walk. The healed man picked up his mat and carried it with him as he walked off to live a new life. Can you imagine his joy at the opportunities that now lay before him? He had been disabled for 38 years. No longer would he depend on others or see them look down their noses at his misfortune; no longer would he wait at the pool for a miracle. This man had been set free from the confines of a badly broken body.

Incredibly, when the Jews saw the healed man carrying his mat, they became upset. They had to have known who this man was. He regularly lay by the Sheep Gate pool, hoping for a chance to enter the stirred waters for the supernatural healing they were believed to provide. Surely they could see this man was now up and walking on his own two legs, something they'd never seen him do before. Surely they saw the miracle right in front of their judgmental faces. Yet they chose to focus their attention on his mat.

In their interpretation, they believed carrying a mat on the Sabbath day to be work, a violation of the law of Moses. In their self-righteous shortsightedness they entirely missed the point; this poor man, disabled for thirty-eight years, could now walk! They couldn't see the miracle in front of them, because their focus was on the law. When they found out Jesus had been the one who healed the man, they took their grievances to Him, outraged at his flagrant dismissal of the law, and charging Him with working on the Sabbath as well.

How arrogant and foolish these men were! Jesus's response encapsulated who He is. He equated Himself with God, saying He and His Father were always working. God is always at work behind the scenes. God hasn't stopped just because we can't see Him or because it's the Sabbath day. God is continually working events out on our behalf in accordance with His plan even when things don't make sense and no matter what day it is.

Is everything subject to God's providence? _____

_____

Have you ever considered your situation to be providential?_____

_____

_____

Have you been able to witness any good come from your situation or from your child's?_____

_____

Can you think of a time when you could clearly see God orchestrating the details of your life?

_____

_____

How can you use the coincidences in your life to point people toward God? _____

_____

_____

Read 1 Peter 1:6–7.

"In all this you greatly rejoice, though now for a little while you may have had to _____
in all kinds of trials. These have come so that the proven genuineness of your _____—of

greater worth than gold, which perishes even though refined by fire—may result in praise, glory, and honor when _____ is revealed."

What is the ultimate good that is supposed to emerge from our sufferings? _____
_____

Have you continued to praise God despite your trials?_____
_____

What is revealed in us through our trials? _____
_____

Whatever our trials, whatever our sufferings, God allows them and uses them to strengthen our faith and to help form our character so it is more in line with Jesus. Which means, though we may vehemently object to them, our trials make us better people.

When you think of the attributes of Jesus, what comes to your mind?_____
_____
_____

Did you list patient, compassionate, and servant-minded? What about holy, loving, and just? When I think of Jesus, those are just a few of the attributes that immediately come to mind. There are so many more I could list! Jesus was perfect; any good and noble attributes found in a person's character are fully epitomized in Jesus Christ.

When you want a picture of love, look to Jesus.
When you want a picture of grace, look to Jesus.
When you want a picture of mercy, look to Jesus.
When you want a picture of kindness, look to Jesus.
When you want a picture of forgiveness, look to Jesus.

Can you see how God has worked in your life through your special needs child to strengthen and grow in you the attributes you listed above?_____

Which one have you grown in the most?_____

Which ones do you still need help with?_____

What steps can you take to help grow your character to be more in line with Jesus? _____
_____

Remember that God chose you to be the parent of a child with unique needs and that everyone is a work in progress. Having a child with special needs involves a continual learning curve. Just take a moment to think of all the growth you've already experienced from having that child in your life. You have most likely changed in many ways you don't even realize. You will continue to be stretched, developing even more the attributes of Jesus as you grow.

Your special needs journey will help you grow in your faith that God is accomplishing good works in you and that He will bring them to a conclusion. Greater good comes out of circumstances that don't seem to be good at first. God is great at flipping a situation upside down, turning dark to light, sadness to joy, and despair to peace.

Read Philippians 1:6.
"Being confident of this, that he who began a _____in you will carry it on to _____ until the day of Christ Jesus."

God is never finished with you. He will provide for you wherever He leads you on your journey. He will guide you, strengthen you, and encourage you. He's entrusted you to travel the long road of special needs parent; trust Him to be your guide.

When your world seems to be spinning uncontrollably, how can you trust that God is actually in control? His sovereignty is there when we look for it. God shows up and He shows us His impressive power; it's found throughout the Bible and it's found in your story too.

What comes to mind when you hear the word *sovereignty?*_____
_____

Merriam-Webster defines *sovereignty* as (1) supreme excellence or an example of it; (2) supreme power with freedom from external control; (3) one that is sovereign, especially an autonomous state.

We often think of sovereignty in relation to countries. A government in a sovereign country has the right to rule the land and people as it pleases, to do whatever it desires without interference from outside sources. God's sovereignty is even broader in scope. God not only has the power and the right to govern but He does so at all times, without exception, over all things. The Creator, because of his creation of all life and all reality, is King of Kings and Lord of Lords. Nothing can thwart Him and

His purpose. He reigns in heaven with the full might of His abilities, with supreme excellence and supreme power, ready to do as He wills. No one can hinder or deter Him. Nothing happens outside God's influence and authority. There is no one like God.

Read Isaiah 46:9–10.

"Remember the former things, those of long ago; I am God, and there is _____ other; I am God, and there is _____ like me. I make known the _____ from the _____, from ancient times, what is still to come. I say: _____ will stand, and I will _____ all that I please."

A powerful account of God's sovereignty is found in the Old Testament story of Nebuchadnezzar, the polytheistic, influential, king of Babylon. He had enormous military and political power. The greatest king in the Babylonian empire, he reigned for more than forty years. We have a lot of historical information about this king. Nebuchadnezzar is even credited with building one of the seven wonders of the ancient world: the Hanging Gardens of Babylon.

Read Daniel 2.

Nebuchadnezzar started having a disturbing dream, the kind that would keep you from wanting to sleep for fear it could happen again. He was greatly troubled by his dream and wanted someone to interpret it for him. But Nebuchadnezzar went a step further and insisted that the interpreter tell him what the dream was before explaining it. If they did not say the dream first, he would cut them into pieces and destroy their home. He was taking no chances. He wanted to make sure no one deceived him about the interpretation. This was a pretty smart idea but a seemingly impossible demand. The king's astrologers told him as much. They told him no one on earth could do as he commanded. No one could tell the king what he dreamed.

What did Nebuchadnezzar dream (Dan. 2:31–35)?_____
_____
_____

Read Daniel 2:11.

"What the kings asks is _____. _____ can reveal it to the king except _____, and they do not live among men."

The king was furious that no one could do what he wanted. He was so irate that he ordered the execution of all the wise men in Babylon. Talk about a power trip! If none of them could interpret his dream, then they were of no use to him alive. To him, their wisdom was just a false pretense.

One of the wise men happened to be a captive from Judah, a godly man named Daniel. While in captivity, Daniel had been educated and trained for service to the king, all the while remaining faithful to God by refusing to defile himself with Babylon's idolatry (Dan. 1:8). Even though Daniel had been given a Babylonian name and was forced to live in their pagan culture, he kept his faith and identity as a follower of the God of Israel.

When Daniel learned of the king's horrific plan, he went before Nebuchadnezzar and asked for some time so that he might be able to interpret the dream for him. After gaining the reprieve, Daniel asked his fellow Judean captives to beseech the Lord for mercy so they might be saved (Dan. 2:18).

What did God do for Daniel (2:23)?_____
_____

Why do you think God allowed a pagan king, who was bullying God's people, to get his way?
_____

God gave Daniel the ability he needed to save all of the wise men in Babylon. God revealed the dream to Daniel and interpreted it for him, and Daniel then revealed this information to Nebuchadnezzar. After Daniel shared the knowledge God had shown him, the king made a wise declaration about Daniel's God.

Read Daniel 2:46–47.
"Then King Nebuchadnezzar fell prostrate before Daniel and paid him honor and ordered that an offering and incense be presented to him. The king said to Daniel, Surely your God is the _____and the _____ and a revealer of mysteries, for you were able to reveal this mystery.'"

What did Nebuchadnezzar's dream mean?_____
_____
_____
_____

What is the final kingdom mentioned in the dream?_____
_____

Nebuchadnezzar, whom Daniel had honored as king of kings, powerful and mighty (2:37), and who was the "head of gold" in the dream (2:38), fell face to the floor in honor of the revelation from the

God of gods. Nebuchadnezzar recognized his kingdom was inferior to the final kingdom that would eventually be established by God. Nebuchadnezzar was in awe of the mysteries revealed and rightly credited God with sovereignty not only over earthly kingdoms but over future history as well. He acknowledged God above all gods and as Lord over all kings. Only a sovereign, omniscient God could reveal future kingdom history hundreds of years in advance, and Nebuchadnezzar knew it.

Even though Nebuchadnezzar praised God's sovereignty, it appears he still didn't fully grasp the truth about who Daniel's God really is. It appears the king believed that the God of the Jews was above all but that there were still other gods worthy of worship. God was willing to take the time to teach Nebuchadnezzar what he needed to learn.

Read Daniel 3.

Nebuchadnezzar remained prideful and arrogant even after witnessing God's authority over time and place, including future events. Suffering from significant egomania, the king put up a gigantic golden statue of himself, and the people were commanded to bow before it when music sounded. To disobey the order would mean death by being thrown into a fire. Nebuchadnezzar thought he was pretty important stuff. He ended up making the statue he had seen in his dream. However, not just the head was made of gold, but the entire statue as well, all ninety feet of it!

Read Daniel 3:15.

"Then what god will be able to _____ you from my hand?"

How short Nebuchadnezzar's memory was! The God of the Jews had just shown His sovereignty over all by allowing Daniel not only to interpret the king's dream but to tell him exactly what he had dreamed. Yet the king of Babylon mocked the thought of a God who could save Shadrach, Meshach, and Abednego. These three men could not bow down before the king's statue because they knew if they did, they would be worshiping the statue as a god or Nebuchadnezzar as a god. They were willing to obey the king as long as they didn't violate God's commandments. They knew there was only one supreme God and wouldn't abandon that belief even in the face of death.

What was the men's response to the command to bow down? _____
_____

The men respectfully told the king that they could not do what he wanted and that if they were thrown into the fire their God could save them. Notice they did not declare that God *would* save them but said they had full confidence that the God of the Jews *could* save them if He wished to do so. He is not just a god; he is *the* God. His sovereignty means it is His prerogative to do as He sees fit. The men acknowledged that and in no uncertain terms they refused to bow down before the statue. This infuriated the king, who had them thrown into the fire at a temperature seven times hotter than normal.

What happened to the men while in the furnace?_____

_____

Who was with the men in the furnace?_____

_____

Remember Nebuchadnezzar's challenge earlier? What god could save the men from the mighty king's hand? Full of himself, Nebuchadnezzar believed that he was sovereign and that what he said would come to pass. However, the true sovereign God showed up while these men were tied up in a super-heated fire. The men were saved from death. Not even one hair on their bodies was singed. No smell of smoke emanated from their clothes. Nebuchadnezzar, in total shock, praised God, calling Him "the Most High God." Without a doubt, the challenge given by the earthly king is met by the sovereignty of the heavenly King.

Read Daniel 4.
Nebuchadnezzar starts off with high praises in recognition of God.

Read Daniel 4:2–3.
"It is my pleasure to tell you about the miraculous signs and wonders that the _____ has performed for me. How _____ are his _____, how _____ His wonders! His _____ is an _____ kingdom; his dominion endures from _____ to _____."

Despite these praises toward God, Nebuchadnezzar still wasn't able to grasp the full sovereignty of the great I Am. After experiencing another disturbing dream, the king summoned Daniel to interpret for him once again. Daniel became greatly concerned at the warning he saw in the dream. He realized this was not good news, and yet he had to explain it to the king. Nebuchadnezzar's royal status was in great danger unless he repented.

What was this new dream about?_____

What does verse 25 say the king needs to do? _____

_____

Did Nebuchadnezzar heed the warnings in the dream?_____

_____

What happened to him?_____

_____

The great king of Babylon suffered the ultimate humiliation. He was brought low, lost his kingly status, and behaved in a wholly undignified way. He spent seven years suffering from some strange malady that prevented him from being his proud, noble self. The warning in Nebuchadnezzar's dream had come to pass and God's sovereignty is once again shown to the lowly king.

Read Daniel 4:34–35.
What verbs are used to describe Nebuchadnezzar's actions?_____

_____

How did he describe God's kingdom?_____

_____

How did he describe God?_____

_____

God's providence and sovereignty are beautifully illustrated in the story of the Babylonian king. Nebuchadnezzar was recorded as a brutal, ambitious ruler who thought highly of himself. He had conquered Judah, had destroyed Jerusalem, and had deported its people to Babylon. He had taken God's people captive. He was powerful and he knew it. He thought he was pretty big stuff. But the truth of almighty God's sovereignty was brought powerfully into focus during Nebuchadnezzar's reign when his kingship was stripped from him. God showed the pagan king that He alone has power over all earthly kingdoms. By divine right God allows rulers to be brought into positions of authority. Nebuchadnezzar didn't heed God's warnings, and God used that defiance to showcase His majesty.

Read Psalm 103:19.
"The Lord has _____ his _____ in heaven, and his kingdom _____ over all."

Read Romans 13:1.
"Everyone must submit himself to the governing authorities, for there is _____ authority except that which God _____."

Read Job 42:2.

"I know you can do all things; _____ of yours can be thwarted."

Read Psalm 22:28.

"For the kingdom is the Lord's and he _____ over the nations."

Read Psalm 135:5–6.

"For I know that the Lord is _____, and that our Lord is _____ all gods. Whatever the Lord pleases, He does, in heaven and in earth, in the seas and in all deeps."

Read Daniel 2:21.

"He changes times and seasons; he _____ kings and _____ up others. He gives wisdom to the wise and knowledge to the discerning."

These verses all have the same theme. Our God is in control. He puts people in power. He allows certain people to have authority. Nothing takes place without His knowledge, and nothing can thwart His plans because God is the ultimate governing authority. God has His reasons and His Word teaches us that we can trust His sovereignty.

Read Acts 17:26.

"From one man he made every nation of men, that they should inhabit the whole earth; and he _____ the times set for them and the exact _____ where they should live."

God has chosen you to be the parent of a child with special needs. He set the time and the place for your family. You and your child are not in the position you are in by mistake. You may not have full confidence in your ability to handle where God is calling you; you may feel that your life has been wrecked and that there is no way it's going to work. But don't ever forget that He believes you are capable of living out His calling for you. This may be the most arduous task you will face, but you won't face it alone. He is with you every step of the way. The same God who walked with Adam and Eve in the garden and who gave Moses the strength to lead the Israelites, is the same God that fights for you today. When you don't understand what God is doing, you must cling to His truth. You don't need to know why when you remember God's wisdom is why.

God knew things would get difficult for Joshua and He wanted him to stay confident throughout them (Josh. 1). God told Joshua to be strong and courageous numerous times to give him the confidence he needed to face his upcoming trials. Doubting God's plan is the easy way out. We too need to be strong, courageous, and confident that God has got our backs through it all. The Lord will be with us through our trials, wherever we go.

Read these verses and put your name on the lines. Pray them with confidence over your life today.

Read Joshua 1:9.

"Have I not commanded you, _____? Be strong and courageous. Do not be frightened, and do not be dismayed, for the Lord your God is with you wherever you go."

Read Isaiah 41:10.

"Fear not, for I am with you, _____; be not dismayed, for I am your God; I will strengthen you_____, I will help you_____, I will uphold you with my righteous right hand."

Read Deuteronomy 31:6.

"Be strong and courageous. Do not fear or be in dread of them, for it is the Lord your God who goes with you. He will not leave you or forsake you, _____."

Read Matthew 28:20.

"Teaching them to observe all that I have commanded you, _____. And behold, I am with you always, to the end of the age."

God's sovereignty and providence are littered throughout the Bible and in your story as well. His presence leaves evidence. After a confetti cannon explosion of glitter and paper, you don't notice where all of the confetti has settled because you are too busy trying to clean up the big mess. You will find confetti months and years later, settled deep into the cracks, hidden in unseen places. Sometimes it's hard to see where all God has been in your situation, because He's settled Himself so well into your circumstances, into the cracks and gaps in your broken life, that you forget He's there.

God reveals Himself as the creator, sustainer, and absolute authority over all of creation. Old Testament history shows God uses the good, the bad, and the ugly to display His glory. His presence is everywhere and is evident when we look for Him. Though our circumstances aren't always good, God and His purpose always are.

Group questions

How can you see God's sovereignty in your life?_____

_____

Is there anything God is not sovereign over?_____

_____

Can you live outside God's purpose for your life?_____

_____

Can you thwart God's plan for your life?_____

_____

Week 2 notes

_____
_____
_____
_____
_____
_____
_____
_____
_____
_____

Jen's Journal

July 30

Many years ago I was asked to lead a support group for parents of special needs kids. I categorically refused and didn't think of it again. There was no way I could do something like that. I was not willing to lead others through their journeys when I needed some serious leading myself.

Years later, as I was talking to a friend, I felt a nudge in the back of my mind about the idea of a support group and how beneficial it might be to belong to one. The next day I called our pastor to see if he would be open to letting someone (not me) lead a group at the church. I figured I could help set one up and participate easily enough, but I had no desire to be the leader. I left a message on our pastor's voicemail and went about my day. That evening I received two phone calls five minutes apart: one from the pastor saying he would love to have me lead a group and the second from someone I hadn't spoken with in years: the person who had originally asked me to lead a support group all those years before. She wanted to know if I would reconsider.

I cannot explain this away as coincidence. The odds against it are ridiculous. I knew God was directly involved, manipulating timelines and events, conversations and thoughts. I knew He was making it crystal clear that I was the one He wanted to lead the support group. Why He chose me I have no clue, but coincidences like that don't just happen. God was all over this entire situation. How kind of my Father's heart to let me say absolutely not and then to nudge me years later to let me know it was time. I had done a lot of growing up in the subsequent years, and while I still didn't like the idea of being the leader, I knew God had matured me and had provided the push I needed to get me out of my comfort zone and into His service.

Come, see a man who told me everything I ever did.

JOHN 4:29

Week 3

Grieving What Could Have Been

The Lord is close to the brokenhearted; He rescues those whose spirits are crushed.
—Psalm 34:18

Introduction

Broken expectations can be the cause of so much of our pain. As the parent of a child with special needs, you might have had to say goodbye to many different things on your journey, things you never would have imagined you'd lose. You might have said goodbye to a clean house, tantrum-free days, socialization, spending time with friends, and spontaneity with your spouse. You might have even said goodbye to financial stability, dreams, friends, church, or possibly even your healthy marriage. Sometimes our life with a special needs child can be very tough, and even just one of these losses would be painful, let alone having to deal with several of them at once. The expectations we created, longed for, and even made goals toward, have vanished like a dandelion puff in the wind.

Do you feel like you are in a perpetual state of grief? Have you let yourself grieve? Grief is a normal and natural, God-given response to pain. There is nothing wrong with grieving the losses in your life. It's painful to let things go, and special needs parents learn to let go of a lot more than average parents do. Our lives are a dizzying series of saying goodbye to one thing while saying hello to something new.

There are five stages to the grief process, according to the Kübler-Ross model, but no two people will grieve the same way, and not everyone will move through all five stages (denial, anger, bargaining, depression, and acceptance). These stages are not linear or universal. Some people will jump around, some will skip a stage, and there is no time frame for reaching the final stage of acceptance. Because no two people grieve the same way, you and your spouse might grieve very differently. If one of you thinks the other isn't grieving anymore, hasn't grieved at all, or didn't grieve long enough, this can add even more stress to an already stressful time in your life.

Grief is not a race to the finish. It is unique to you and to your situation.

People in the Bible experienced grief, and just like us, it could stem from unmet expectations and from losses. We can learn how to move through grief in a healthy way that will keep us looking forward instead of dwelling on the shoulda, woulda, couldas of our life.

God can and will use our grief in a powerful way to bring us closer to Him. This week let us pray for the healing rescue of our broken hearts and ask God to gather us near, helping us feel secure under the shelter of His wings.

> "Many are the plans in the mind of a man, but it is the purpose of the Lord that will stand" (Prov. 19:21).

I love the book of Ruth. We can all relate to this wonderful story of a woman's hope and ultimate redemption. There are no angels sweeping in with news, no miraculous events, and no supernatural occurrences involved in her challenges. It's the account of an ordinary woman, facing difficult, almost insurmountable problems, with the support of family. We can learn so much from Ruth's experience. It provides another example of how God moves and orchestrates events in the lives of regular people, just like you and me, and how He makes beautiful things come from the harshest beginnings.

Let's take a look at the story of Naomi and Ruth.

Read Ruth 1:1–5.
Who was Naomi? _____

Naomi and her husband were Hebrews. During the time of the book of Judges, Israel had suffered a severe famine. Naomi's story takes place during this period. Her husband, Elimelech, decided to move his family away from Bethlehem instead of weathering out the famine in their homeland. The family traveled to the town of Moab, perhaps some sixty miles away from their home. Elimelech chose to take his family to a heathen land, apparently in search of a better life, but it was a dangerous alternative. This would have been a very difficult transition for these faith-filled people due to the Moabites' pagan beliefs. The family was in direct disobedience of God's orders; His people were to stay away from the Moabites.

What happened to Naomi's husband and two sons while they were in Moab?_____

How do you think Naomi felt? _____
_____

We don't know how long after moving to Moab Naomi's husband died, but we know that ten years after marrying Moabite women, both of Naomi's sons died as well. The main problem for Naomi was that she was left alone with no husband and no sons. She was now destitute. This would have been a terrifying and traumatic situation for her. The protection and livelihood guaranteed to the widowed matriarch of the family by her sons had vanished with their deaths. Widowed women needed protection and care from a male relative or benefactor to survive. The thing any widowed woman would fear had happened; Naomi was left without anyone to provide for her, and to top it off, she was in a foreign land. She had no extended family to count on.

Read Ruth 1:6–10.
What prompted Naomi to leave Moab?_____

Who went with her?_____

How did Naomi's daughters-in-law respond to her desire to return to her homeland? _____

Why did Naomi send her daughters-in-law away? _____
_____

Read Ruth 1:10–13.
Naomi started to move through the stages of the grief cycle at this point. Remember, we don't necessarily hit all the stages; each person moves through grief differently.

What does this passage reveal about Naomi's heart and mind?_____
_____

Naomi felt that God had placed a judgment upon her. She wanted her daughters-in-law to head back home. Naomi felt she was suffering the bitter consequences of the choice her family made to leave the Hebrew people and to live in the forbidden land of Moab. Her daughters-in-law could safely return to their people and be cared for there by their families. But there was no family for Naomi and no hope for a future in Moab. She didn't want them to have to undergo what she would soon be experiencing.

Read Ruth 1:16–17.

How did Ruth's attitude differ from Naomi's? _____

_____

Ruth, Naomi's daughter-in-law, desired to stay with her and pledged loyalty to Naomi, for as long as she lived. Ruth made a commitment, that no matter what the future held, she would choose Naomi's God to be her God and she would never leave her. Ruth clearly had a deep love for Naomi and didn't want to abandon her to whatever future awaited her back home. The two journeyed on to Bethlehem where Naomi met up with her fellow people, whom she had not seen in well over a decade. What should have been a wonderful homecoming, a joyous reunion, was tainted by her pain.

Read Ruth 1:19–21.

Why did Naomi tell her people not to call her by her given name? _____

_____

What did she tell them to call her? _____

Why? _____

_____

How do you think Naomi felt at this point? _____

_____

Can you relate in any way to how Naomi felt? _____

_____

In these verses we get a better glimpse of what Naomi was feeling down in her heart. The name Naomi means "pleasant," and the name Mara means "bitter." Naomi's heart had been crushed; she was broken in spirit. Her decision to change her name could have been motivated by grief, anger, sorrow, or a combination of them all. Naomi told her people to call her Mara from now on, a name she felt reflected God's judgment upon her life. She was outwardly marking herself with what she believed was God's punishment passed down to her. She wanted to be known by her pain. Naomi was not in a good mental or emotional place at this point. Her life used to be pleasurable, but now it was painful. She was grieving over what she had lost and for her bleak future. Her outlook was bitter, her attitude was bitter, so her name might as well be bitter too.

Read Ruth 2:2.

Who went out into the field to gather leftovers from the harvest?_____

Why do you think she went alone? _____

_____

It's significant that Ruth, a young Moabite widow, and all alone, took the initiative to go out into the barley field to try to provide for both of them. Naomi appeared to be in a stage of depression in which she was suffering from loneliness and fatigue. She was submerged in her isolation and wasn't looking forward or taking any responsibility to help provide for their well-being. Naomi seemed to be wallowing in despair, unable to think ahead even to the basics of food. It would have been dangerous for Ruth, a foreigner, to gather food alone. It was hot and hard work and sometimes women were taken advantage of. Ruth was not of the people. The Moabites were people the Hebrews were to avoid. Naomi would have known of the dangers, and yet she allowed Ruth to go out alone. Naomi couldn't even think clearly enough to care for and to protect Ruth.

Have you experienced grief or depression like Naomi's and found you couldn't think beyond the next moment?_____

_____

Did you have anyone in your life to help you move through your grief?_____

_____

Whether your help came from the Lord or from someone else, have you been able to help others in their grief with the help you received? _____

_____

Read Ruth 3:1–5.

What did Naomi say she needed to get for Ruth? _____

What did Naomi tell Ruth to do?_____

_____

_____

Naomi seemed to finally be thinking forward to the future. She was over her despondency and depression and she was no longer living moment to moment. She wasn't sitting idly in her grief and isolation, watching life pass her by. She was hatching a plan to secure a life for Ruth hoping to get her a husband. She showed a renewed focus and hope for the future and finally felt a duty toward Ruth. Naomi had determination and a renewed sense of purpose.

What did Ruth say she would do?_____

Read Ruth 4:13–17.

What was Naomi's attitude at this point?_____

How had Naomi's future changed?_____

_____

Ruth and Boaz, a relative of Elimelech, Naomi's husband, eventually married. This kinsman redeemer secured the future of Naomi's faithful daughter-in-law and of Naomi herself. Naomi completed her grief cycle with acceptance, hope, and a fullness of new life. What seemed at first to be a story of brokenness turns into a story of blessing. Naomi got to cherish and nurture her grandson, Obed, who would become the grandfather of the great King David.

We witness in Naomi's story a cycle of pain and despair that we can all relate to. Unmet expectations, death, loss of income, loss of home, hopelessness, and depression are all real-life occurrences for us special needs families too. But we have an advantage that Naomi didn't have when she was in the midst of her grief. We know how her story ends. We get to see the bigger picture of her life and its impact. We get to see the good that came out of the bad. We get to see God's providence. Redemption took place through Naomi's story because King David came from her family line. God took a woman whose husband and sons had died, ending her genetic line, and He grafted her family on to the family tree of Abraham. God placed her in the family line of King David and ultimately of Jesus!

Looking through Naomi's story reveals God's glory. Your story is the same! Things don't always turn out how we plan them, but they will turn out how God plans them, because His purpose is greater and woven into every aspect.

I want us to take another look at Job this week. The stories of Job and Naomi have happy endings. We get to see the beauty that came from their tragedies and to understand the deeper meaning found in what they endured on their journeys. But remember, they didn't have foresight to know how their futures would turn out. They had to live and move through their pain with each passing day bringing more grief and more uncertainty just like we do.

When we visited Job in the first chapter we looked at his story in the context of whether we should ask God, "Why me?" Let's focus now on how Job's journey mirrors a grief cycle similar to Naomi's.

Remember, Job suffered through an unbelievable night as servant after servant reported tremendous tragedies befalling his livestock, his servants, and then his children. By the end of the evening Job was left with a devastating new reality. The only tangible things left in his life were his wife and his home. What a shock to his system to have just one of these tragedies befall him, but all of them in one day? What a nightmare he was forced to endure.

Read Job 1:21.

"Naked I came from my mother's womb, and naked I will_____. The Lord_____ and the Lord has _____; may the name of the Lord be_____."

How did Job respond initally?_____
_____

Job would have been in a severe state of shock at first. Nonetheless he was straightforward in his proclamation that God gives and takes away and he praised the name of the Lord. This initial praise and thanksgiving to God for what he had been given would have been an automatic inclination for anyone with Job's deep and abiding faith. His praise for the Creator of the things that were taken from him testified to Job's understanding of who made them all in the first place. Job knew his place. You are never more aware of your inability to control your life than when you realize that control was just an illusion and you were never in charge at all; you've been back seat driving thinking you had the wheel the entire time.

Read Job 3.

Job's war of words begin at this point in his story. He goes on a long rant about wishing the day of his birth didn't exist. He laments about how that day should be cursed. I love how we get to see the depth of Job's anguish. He doesn't hold back his feelings. He exposes his heart and cries out for mercy with every ounce of energy he has left. His body may not have been functioning, but his mouth sure was, and he was going to use it.

What benefits did Job ascribe to the different classes of people who have died?

The wealthy kings?_____

A stillborn infant?_____

The wicked and the weary?_____

Captives?_____

Ultimately, all of these people have been freed from the confines of their earthly bodies and they are now at peace. Death is the great equalizer. Even the kings who caused great difficulties and calamities are fully at rest in their graves. These people experience no more toil, no more pain, and no more troubles. There is no more earthly strife no matter their status. Death, in Job's mind, would be a reprieve from his feelings. He could experience relief. He would be freed from his pain.

What irony did Job speak of in verses 20–23?_____
_____
_____

In deliberate contrast with Job's life experience was his testament to why good things happen to bad people. He asked why those who long for death are not taken while those who are in misery receive reprieves. He asked why life is granted to someone who can't even enjoy it. We've all asked these questions. Why do such stark contrasts exist in this life?

Read Job 7:11–16.
Now we see Job's anger materialize. He struggled with his sufferings and wrestled with his emotions. He asked if he was the sea that needed to be hedged in or a monster that needed confinement. Those are bold visualizations of violent forces. Was Job so awful God had to limit him?

"Therefore I will not keep silent; I will speak out in the _____, I will _____ in the _____ of my soul" (v. 11).

"I _____ my life, I would not live forever. _____; my days have no meaning" (v. 16).

Read Job 9:33–34.
Job started to imagine bargaining with God. Could a mediator intervene since God wasn't responding?

"If only there were someone to _____ between us, to lay his hand upon us both, someone to remove God's rod from me, so that his terror would frighten me no more."

Read Job 10:18.
Job's depression becomes evident. He loathes his very life and feels God created him for no reason.

"Why then did you bring me out of the womb? I _____ before any eye saw me."

Read Job 13:15.
Job finally found acceptance. He has learned to keep hope in God even when doubts arise.

"Though he slay me, _____ hope in him."

After a long conversation in which God reprimanded Job and reminded him that his problems and sufferings were not paramount in the universe, Job responded, "Surely I spoke of things I did not understand, things too wonderful for me to know" (Job 42:3).

Job moved back and forth between the five stages of grief throughout the entirety the book. Before gaining a level of acceptance, Job wished he'd never been born (the closest a traditional Jew could appropriately come to verbalizing sacrilegious suicidal thinking), wished he could have an audience with God in order to negotiate with Him, and exploded at God for His injustice and for the inadequate comfort He offered. These stages were repeated and sometimes intermingled. We don't know how much time passed while Job suffered and tried to grapple with his new reality. At one point, he mentioned months, so it's safe to say he spent a serious amount of time working through his grief. Job lived day to day with unknowns, shifting his feelings, taking the major detour in his life unwillingly to its next stop until he finally realized he desired God more than any earthly pleasures.

Do you feel like you have moved through the stages of grief in the face of your child's diagnosis? ___
_____
_____

Have you and your spouse grieved differently, causing confusion and misunderstanding of each other's feelings?_____
_____

Please hear me on this: Allow yourself ample time to mourn and to weep. Allow yourself to move through the stages of grief at your own pace, and remember everyone grieves differently. It is okay for you and your spouse to be at different stages and to move through them at differing speeds. Keeping this in mind will help you when you feel like the two of you are not on the same page. You probably aren't! And that is perfectly all right. How we show grief differs from person to person and woman to man. Some of us may need to isolate ourselves, some seek connection, some want to talk things out, while others need to keep themselves busy. Each of these things is normal and does not mean one person is experiencing grief any less than another.

Grief is a nasty, tricky thing. You may feel like you have moved on and when you least expect it, grief will suddenly reappear, tearing your heart back open on what you thought was a long ago healed and hardened scar. Something will trigger it; a smell may take you back to the hospital, a thought long lost will resurface, your child's peers will celebrate milestones your child won't, new diagnoses will be attached to your child, and before you know it you are back rolling in sorrow. It can be frustrating to revisit feelings you thought had long since been healed or buried. Grief will eventually drop by less often and will not linger as long. Putting our hope in a providential God we can fully trust will help us when we wrestle with our losses. May we be like Job and confidently state, "Though He slay me, yet will I hope in Him."

How can you draw close to God in your grief instead of feeling like He is far from you? When you get sucked into the pain, you can easily forget how much He loves you. These verses are meant to remind you that God is never far from you. Commit them to memory, or place them on note cards in your home so you can be reminded that God is the great comforter, and He will never leave you.

Read Psalm 34:18.
"The Lord is _____ to the brokenhearted and saves those who are crushed in spirit."

Read Psalm 147:3.
"He _____ the brokenhearted and binds up their wounds."

Read Joshua 1:9.
"Have I not commanded you? Be strong and courageous. So not be terrified, do not be discouraged, for the Lord your God will be _____ wherever you go."

Read Matthew 5:4.
"Blessed are those who mourn, for they _____."

Read 2 Corinthians 1:3–4.
"Blessed be to the God and Father of our Lord Jesus Christ, the Father of _____ and the God of all _____ who comforts us in our _____ so that we can comfort those in any troubles with the comfort we ourselves have received from God."

God tells us over and over that He is with us in our troubles, in our grief, and that He will not abandon us. Scripture tells us to cast all of our anxieties on Him because He cares for us (1 Peter 5:7). We cannot change what has happened in our lives that brought us to where we are now, but we can focus on moving forward through our grief. We can allow our trials to bring us closer to God revealing our dependence on Him, trusting that our experiences can be used to help others in their need, and that troubles can ultimately be used to bring God glory if we allow it. God wastes nothing.

Write John 11:35. _____

When we suffer sorrow, we should take great comfort in this verse because we witness Jesus modeling grief for us. Though He knew He would raise Lazarus from the dead, Jesus shared in Martha's and Mary's grief and empathized with them. He felt their pain, He felt their sorrow, and He grieved their loss. He had such compassion for what they were experiencing that he wept with them. Jesus could have told them, "Don't grieve. Just wait. I'm going to do something amazing soon that will take away your pain." Instead, He sank down with them in the moment and shared the sorrow they bore.

It's okay to grieve your losses, the shoulda, woulda, couldas of your life. God gave us tears to mourn in our pain. We cry because we hurt. This life is full of uncomfortable things at every turn. But Jesus didn't turn away when trouble came. He met pain head-on, with a heart full of love that overflowed unto His death. He moved through suffering despite His pain, abandoning the outcome to God's will. God wants the very same for us. Sometimes God takes us through heartache to help us let go of things that were never ours to hold on to in the first place.

Group questions

What things have you had to bid farewell? _____

_____

Do you see any parallels in your life with the way Ruth and Job experienced the cycle of grief? _____

_____

Were you able to respond with the faith-filled perspective of Job when you found out about your child's special needs?_____

_____

Does understanding that all people grieve differently help you in your relationship with your spouse and with how your spouse has handled their grief or acceptance of your situation? _____

_____

Have you experienced a moment when the grief came flooding back unexpectedly?_____

_____

_____

Week 3 notes

_____

_____

_____

_____

_____

_____

_____

_____

_____

Jen's Journal

I'm not a good griever. Is *griever* even a real word? I'm not good at goodbyes and I don't like sadness. Grief is both of those combined and on steroids. No one is immune from death and goodbyes. I know that. No one can escape this life without experiencing some depth of sadness. But I don't like it and I prefer not to experience it. At all. Not ever. I'm not even a good comforter in someone else's grief. I feel super sucky at it.

I never thought I could be any more sadder than when I buried my stillborn daughter. But then I buried my son's twin brother nine months later. Life was difficult. Anguish was my companion. Showering took too much thought processing. Makeup was for people who had their lives together. Hair? Who cares about vanity when your children lie cold in their coffins? Meals were a snack pack of chips and crackers washed down with a can of Dr Pepper. Every breath was painful. I lived in fear of my surviving twin son passing at any moment. I refused to plan his funeral, in case I would have to put both my babes in the coffin. Everyone was sad and felt sorry for me, and that made me even more depressed. I didn't want their sympathy. I wanted my son. I wanted my daughter. My husband couldn't fix my grief, and knowing how much he loves to fix things made me all the more saddened. Nothing would ever be the same. Nothing could fix this nightmare. My old life, my old innocence, was gone. How would I fill the hole in my soul? I would never be the same.

But God, my friends. But God. He reached out, throwing me a lifeline in the middle of my raging storm. He pulled me up out of the water to the safety of His love. He allowed me to see that joy could and would eventually be a part of my life again. Meeting me amid the wracked sobs after my son's death, God give me a sign of hope.

After Brady's funeral, I was full on blubbering so hard I couldn't can't catch my breath. Tears and snot were streaming down my face. I went to blow my nose, and as I put the tissue up to my face, a huge sob escaped from deep inside of me, causing me to suddenly take in air. When I inhaled I sucked the tissue right into the very back of my throat. The sound I made as I gasped for air and tried to spit out the tissue was nothing short of magnificent. I sputtered and spat, trying to get all of the instantly dissolved pieces of tissue out of my mouth and off of my tongue. Then I burst out laughing, a full belly laugh. The stupidity of how I looked and what had just happened gave me a huge case of the giggles. I'd just inhaled tissue in a deep, heart-wrenching sob, and I was so grateful for the moment. I felt God interrupt my deep sorrow and lift me from the valley of the shadow of death. He was reminding me that I would be happy again. The moment brought some much-needed levity to my broken heart and my weary soul. My tears of sadness turned into tears of laughter.

I know that moment was a precious gift from God. It sounds so silly to some, I know. My heartache was so intense and my grief so overwhelming, but when I sucked in that tissue, grief's hold was broken. I got a chance to reset. And I love the fact that God gave me the opportunity to experience such deep sorrow and silly joy at the same time. He rescued me. That's the kind of God we serve—one who loves us so much He shows up in the grief to let us know that everything will be okay, that we will experience laughter again, that joy will come in the mourning!

"Even in laughter the heart may ache" (Prov. 14:13).

Many are the plans in a man's heart, but it is the Lord's purpose that prevails.

Proverbs 19:21

Week 4

Disability, Brokenness, and Suffering

I am different but not less.

—Temple Grandin

Introduction

I'm excited we have finally arrived at the week in our study where we can dig in and explore the topic of disability! It's the unifying factor that has brought all of us to this study. It impacts our lives on a daily basis and we want to learn more about what God thinks concerning the subject. Why does God allow some people to be disabled, to be weaker members of society? Why does God allow special needs? Why doesn't He fix these problems? Does He create people with disabilities? Why would a good God do that? Does He think less of people with disabilities?

I think we have a lot of misinformation and misconceptions about God and His role in disabilities. He does not view anyone with special needs as "less than". We humans have done that all on our own. We are the ones with the distorted views of worth. We are the ones who have equated value with performance. Everyone is important to God and he loves and values everyone the same. What we so easily forget is that all of us are imperfect in one way or another: emotionally, intellectually, or socially. Some people's imperfections are readily visible, while others can hide theirs inside, but all of us fall far short of perfection and are fundamentally broken inside. No one is perfect, and God views us all through the same lens.

Not only do we see numerous people who are broken and imperfect throughout the Bible, but we read about actual physical disabilities: palsy, paralysis, blindness, deafness, and disabling diseases. How can we convince others and ultimately ourselves to see beyond disabilities to the value of the person inside unless we try to fully understand God's view? We can learn a lot about ourselves and those with disabilities when we learn more about what God has to say. Let's cast cultural views to the side and embrace God's standard of value.

Lord, we ask for wisdom this week as we learn to embrace our own flaws and brokenness in order to help ourselves and others embrace our children with special needs.

> "As the heavens are higher than the earth, so are my ways higher than your ways and my thoughts than your thoughts" (Isa. 55:9).

For the sake of practicality and because it has so many associations, let's define the word *disabled*.

What does *disabled* mean to you? What immediately comes to mind?_____
_____

If we're really honest, the majority of us would define *disabled* as an inability to function the way the human body is physically designed to function. We tend to think of someone who is physically abnormal, someone whose disabilities are obvious. Most people immediately think of a disabled person as one with more demanding physical needs, someone in a wheelchair. After all, the universal symbol for disability is a blue icon of a person in a wheelchair. Most of us are going to naturally think of a disabled person as someone with physical needs.

According to *Merriam-Webster, disabled* means "incapacitated by illness or injury; also: physically or mentally impaired in a way that substantially limits activity especially in relation to employment or education."

The term *disabled* carries many different meanings when used to describe people in spite of its limited dictionary definition. A person with a back injury that prevents him from standing for long periods is labeled disabled just as a person confined to a wheelchair and requiring total care is labeled disabled. You can argue that one is less disabled than the other, that one is affected more significantly than the other, and while that is true, they both carry the label of disabled. Their disabilities look totally different and affect their lives in completely different ways, but according to definition they both bear the same defining label.

The Americans with Disabilities Act defines a disabled person as one who has a physical or mental impairment that substantially limits one or more major life activities, someone who has a history or record of such an impairment, or who is perceived by others as having such an impairment.

This official definition is supposed to offer a more precise description of what a disability entails, but it still leaves a lot of room for interpretation. It's difficult to define the many disabilities we see based on this definition alone.

Now let's define *broken*.

What does *broken* mean to you?_____
_____

When you think of *broken*, do you think of something that doesn't work at all? Or do you think of something that still works despite its flaws?

According to *Merriam-Webster*, *broken* means "damaged or altered by or as if by breaking; made weak or infirm; not complete or full."

A toy with a broken button can still function; your child can still play with the toy just fine. You can break your glasses but still be able to use them to see. You can break an arm and still function even though the arm is unusable. What about emotional or psychological scars that leave you feeling broken? They can affect you and possibly your relationships, but you remain a functional human being; you can still go about your daily life. What about mental illness and mentally disabling conditions that aren't so obvious from the outside, the ones that keep people from living in freedom? All of these examples of brokenness have one thing in common: effectiveness. These people and things can still be used despite their flaws. The same goes for the broken people in the Bible. These were individuals whom God used despite their physical appearance and in spite of the brokenness and damage to their hearts, souls, and lives.

Do you think of broken or weak people as being disabled?_____
_____

Why or why not?_____
_____
_____

The Bible shows God using broken, weak, and disabled people to reveal His grace and mercy, to fulfill His plans, and to showcase His unlimited power. He used physical or personality flaws for His sovereign purposes time and time again.

Moses was a murderer with a speech problem.

David was a coveter and a murderer.

Gideon was afraid and unsure.

Jeremiah suffered depression.

Samson was a womanizer.

Jonah ran away from God.

Rahab was a prostitute.

Martha was a worrier.

Paul was a persecutor.

Elijah was suicidal.

Peter was a liar.

Why does God use so many unexpected people through out history? Why are the power players of God's story full of so many issues? Why are so many flawed people highlighted in the Bible? Let's look at a few scripture passages, keeping this idea of broken, flawed, and disabled people in mind.

Read Exodus 4:10–12.

Moses objected to God using him. What did Moses think the problem was?_____

_____

_____

Moses considered himself to have a handicap. He viewed himself as flawed and he complained about his speech. He clearly had an issue with the way he spoke, whether it was an inability to enunciate properly or to articulate his thoughts well. We don't know exactly what the issue was, but it was significant enough to Moses that he felt completely inadequate when God called on him. Whatever the impediment was, it prevented Moses from being able to boldly and confidently speak in public, and he felt it significantly limited his ability to take on the role God had assigned to him. Moses didn't think he was good enough and he objected to God using him.

God immediately rebuked Moses's objections. God could not care less that Moses thought himself inadequate. God created Moses and knew what he was capable of. He reminded Moses of this fact with what some might consider a surprising statement.

"The Lord said to him, 'Who gave man his_____? Who makes him _____or
_____? Who gives him _____ or makes him _____?'"

What did God say He does? _____

_____

God took credit for creating some people with certain disabilities. Does this surprise you? _____

_____

Obviously not all disabilities come directly from God. We have free will that allows us to make poor choices, resulting in poor outcomes. Accidents and injuries that are entirely our fault can produce disabling conditions. But I feel it's important to grasp what God is saying here, because it might be a bit shocking at first. He told Moses that He makes people blind and deaf, that the issues some people face come directly from Him! There can be some debate among scholars whether God means He creates people *with* disabilities or creates people who *get* disabilities. Because of that argument, let's compare what God said to Moses in the Old Testament with what Jesus said in the New Testament.

Read John 9:1–3.
"As he passed by, he saw a man blind from birth. And his disciples asked him, 'Rabbi, who sinned, this_____ that he was born blind?' Jesus answered, 'It was _____ this _____ or his _____, but that the _____ of _____ might be _____ in him.'"

What was Jesus saying about this blind man?_____

_____

God created man, yet due to the fall in the garden of Eden, we see many imperfections in humanity today. We see deafness, blindness, disease, disorders, and genetic conditions. We are the furthest from perfect any society has ever been. But according to Jesus's own words, which parallel what God told Moses from the burning bush, God allows, even creates, disabilities. God purposely permits disabilities in certain people for a greater display of His glory.

Jesus was doing something here that needs a little bit of back story. He was responding, in part, to a popular misconception. The Jewish belief at the time was that all defects or disabilities were the direct result of a sin by the affected person or by that person's parents. Jews believed that disability was a judgment from God and that there was direct correlation between sin and disability. They assumed this man was born blind as the direct result of sin.

While sin came into the world directly through the fall of man, Jesus was saying this man's disability was not a direct punishment for sin. Jesus told His disciples there was a divine purpose beyond what they saw at face value in this man. They were sure that this man had somehow suffered due to sin and that he had caused his own blindness, but Jesus told them something they never expected to hear. This blind man had a purpose, a mission, that was far more valuable than they could imagine and that went beyond their beliefs and expectations. He was not disabled due to sin but so that God could be glorified.

Has anyone ever blamed you for your child's special needs?_____
_____

Have you blamed yourself in any way for your child's disabilities?_____
_____

Does knowing that God creates people with certain disabilities make it easier for you to accept the situation your child has been given? _____
_____
_____

Your answer might be a resounding no if you are recently into a diagnosis. At the onset of challenges it's hard to see that they could be used for anything good. Our first response is usually shock or denial. God has chosen to allow you, your family, and your child to face an issue that will not always be easy. Why does He allow this to happen to us? What purpose can be served by our suffering? God rarely does things the way we expect Him to. In fact, if we had our own way, trials, trouble, and pain would never enter into our lives. We would take the reins of our lives and trot along at a pace of our own choosing. But God tells us to hold on tight because He's got a new trail for us to blaze at a galloping speed. With much obstinacy, we usually pull back on the reins so we don't get hurt. But God never calls us to be safe. He never guarantees us an easy path. God never calls trailblazers to take the easy road.

How many times does God use people who by society's standards would seem too weak to bring about His plan and His glory? He does it time and time again. David, Gideon, and Joseph, historical heroes of the Old Testament, were weak and undeniably flawed people. Name almost any major biblical character and you can find a flaw.

Read 1 Samuel 16:6–13.
"Do not consider his _____ or his _____, for I have rejected him. The Lord _____. Man looks on the outward appearance, but the Lord looks at the _____."

God is telling us that He sees beyond what we see and that we should quit taking things at face value. He told Samuel that the automatic inclination to judge by the outward appearance is extremely foolish and shortsighted. God had chosen David, the baby brother living in the shadow of his older siblings. He wanted the least in the family, the one not even worth inviting in from the fields when the prophet came to visit. God wasn't impressed by the good looks or the height of David's older brothers. He didn't choose them on their appearance, their birth order, or their skills. God desired the one society would have considered last of all, because He saw something different in him. He saw his heart.

God continually uses the least expected to bring about His plan. Our inadequacies allow God to show off the impressive things He can do with so little. Our all-knowing God always sees beyond what we can see with our limited vision and opinionated assumptions. God knows what we are capable of, where our journey will take us, and what we will experience getting there. What hope that is for us when we feel weak, overlooked, damaged, and underappreciated! God doesn't see us or our children the way the world does, our outward appearance is irrelevant to Him.

Read Judges 6:11–16.
"But Lord," Gideon asked, "how can I save Israel? My _____ is the _____ in Manasseh and I am _____ in my family."

Here God again chose another youngest sibling, of a tribe that was least in its community, to show His might and His glory through the least expected. Gideon was afraid. He was hiding out during wartime by threshing wheat in a small, confined space, not in one of the typically large, fully exposed locations normally used. Gideon didn't want to be seen by anyone, and yet God saw him. It is in this hidden-away spot that an angel appeared to Gideon and said the Lord was sending him to fight to save Israel.

What was Gideon's reaction? He wasn't feeling very brave that's for sure. He was in disbelief. He was shocked. How could such an insignificant man be the one to fight so mightily for the Lord? How could he have been chosen to bring God glory? Gideon was not a leader. He wasn't physically mighty. Gideon wasn't even the privileged firstborn son. He was last in line in his family and from the weakest tribe, but despite all of his shortcomings, God called him to battle.

Why do you think God uses the least, the weak, the unexpected, and the broken for His purposes?

_____

_____

Read 1 Corinthians 1:27.

"But God _____ the foolish things of the world to shame the wise; God chose the _____ of the world to _____."

God is thrilled to use the broken, the weak, and the forgotten to reproach the wise and to disgrace the strong for a bigger plan and greater purpose than we can immediately see. God takes great delight in using the unexpected. Try to imagine the Bible full of perfect people, living perfect lives and doing everything perfectly. Not only is that unrealistic and impossible to relate to, but the flaws of its people show just how trustworthy the Bible is! If men wanted to create God and to write about Him and His people, they surely wouldn't have filled the pages of history with people of such questionable character. But that's exactly what we see. We see God using average, unsavory, broken, or disabled people to achieve miraculous and amazing things, not through their own power but through the power of God.

Read 1 Corinthians 12:22.

"On the contrary, those parts of the body that seem to be _____ are_____."

What is Paul saying in this verse?_____

_____

How does this apply to people with disabilities and special needs? _____

_____

_____

Paul paints a picture of the body of believers in Jesus Christ: the church. He says we will have some who seem less integral to the church but are actually just as important as the major parts. People many may view as undesirable or of less value, who don't fit in or don't belong, are actually indispensable for the necessary function of the entire body of Christ. No one part is greater than another. Preconceived notions that people with fewer skills and abilities bring nothing of value to the church, and ultimately to God, is flat-out wrong. Paul argues that diversity in the body of Christ is to be expected and is a necessary component of God's work in and through His people. Weaker parts of the body are absolutely vital for a fully functioning church.

In the past, society tended to have a tainted view of disabilities. People would be judged, marginalized, and even hidden away. And while huge strides have been made in gaining acceptance of people with special needs, more work still needs to be done. This is where we parents of special needs kids can focus. We get to show society what Paul means. People with disabilities belong in the church.

We see how amazing our kids are and how beautiful they are *because* they are different. Our kids are an inspiration! We have the honor of showcasing the diversity found in having unique and special needs. Others miss out by not experiencing the love and the beauty we see. As parents and advocates, we can show the world that our kids are marvelous and valuable, and that they matter. We have the privilege of shouting their worth. We need to let their light shine! They may stick out because they are "different" but they belong in society just like everyone else. They belong in our churches too. They may be considered weaker members of the human family in certain aspects, but they are just as much a part of the body of Christ as anyone else. They are unique, invaluable and indispensable and we have so much to learn from them.

How does this knowledge from Paul correlate to the people you see in your local church? _____
_____
_____

How does it relate to your family?_____
_____

God wants everyone to know there is room for them in His church and in His kingdom. He wants everyone there no matter their physical, mental, or emotional limitations. God doesn't want anyone left out just because they feel less than or look different from others. Remember, weaker never means less valuable to God. His focus isn't on what you can provide or on how you look; His focus is on the heart.

Have you ever heard of Mephibosheth? This story of David and his compassion is tucked into 2 Samuel and is considered a prefiguring of the coming of the Messiah. David was very good friends with King Saul's son, Jonathan. They were an example of true friendship and were as close as brothers. They had pledged loyalty to each other.

Read 1 Samuel 20:15
What did Jonathon request of David? _____

Out of jealousy, Saul would eventually want David dead, but David wouldn't return the feeling. David was loyal and would not hurt his friendship with Jonathon nor the position God had given him. When David had the chance to kill Saul, he always chose mercy, letting God be the one to seek retribution on his behalf. David went through terribly difficult experiences with Saul and his family. A lot of us might have washed our hands of Saul's entire clan if we had suffered the way David had. Yet, after all immediate members of the family had died, David was severely heartbroken. He desired to recognize the family in some way. He held much grief over the loss of Saul, Jonathan, and the others and hoped someone was still alive in the family line that he could show kindness to. David wanted to honor his promise to Jonathan.

Read 2 Samuel 9:1–13.

How is Jonathan's son described? _____

Where was this son located? _____

Why do you suppose David didn't know about Jonathan's son? _____

_____

A former servant from Saul's house was called in to give David notice that there was someone remaining in Saul's family to whom he could show some kindness and respect. The servant told David that the man was Jonathan's son and that he was crippled in both feet. In 2 Samuel 4:4 we learn why the man suffered from this disabling condition. At five years of age, he became crippled when his nurse dropped him while fleeing in fear for their lives after hearing that Jonathan, the boy's father, had been killed. This man had been handicapped since he was a young boy due to a freak accident.

The servant didn't even mention the descendant by name but used his defective features to describe him. That's how this man was known, by his disability, not by his nobility as the surviving grandson of King Saul. He was just "the cripple." That was his identity.

When David met Mephibosheth, he told him not to be afraid. David wanted him to know he meant him no harm. Mephibosheth was the closest living relative to Saul and might have feared that David wanted to end the familial line once and for all. Mephibosheth would have known the history of his grandfather and David. He would have known Saul despised David, that he'd hunted him down and tried to kill him. But David told him something completely unexpected. David just wanted to bless him. He told him he wanted to honor Jonathan and Saul by giving the family land back to the family by returning it to him. This incredible and inestimable gift would have given the crippled Mephibosheth security and a future.

Read 2 Samuel 9:8.

"Mephibosheth bowed down and said, 'What is your servant, that you should notice a _____ like me?'"

Mephibosheth referred to himself in a pitiful way. He viewed himself as worthless and equal to a dead dog. He equated himself with an animal that was unclean and was held in contempt by society.

Mephibosheth didn't claim the nobility in his past or pride in his familial line. He could have stood proud of his ancestry, but he holds himself in low esteem and has poor self confidence. He was a significantly disabled man with nothing to offer a king. Society pitied him, maybe even viewed him as a sinner for having the disability befall him.

Notice that Mephibosheth lived in Lo Dabar, which translated from Hebrew means "land of nothing". He lived with a family that was not of his own and he had no heritage. This man with no name came from the land of nothing, had nothing to give, and suffered from a negative self-image. His outlook was thoroughly sad and depressing.

David responded to Mephibosheth's question by ordering Saul's former servant to farm the newly returned family land and to bring in the crops for Mephibosheth. David answered Mephibosheth with action. David showed Mephibosheth that he had worth not only by giving him the land but by having it farmed for him as well.

Then, in an act of ultimate compassion, prefiguring Christ, David invited Mephibosheth to dine at his table—the king's table. Even with his visible disability, Mephibosheth would always be welcome to eat with the king, with nobility, just as if he were David's own son. David gave this broken man hope and a future. He gave him back his dignity. He gave him safety, security, and abundance. David sought after Mephibosheth out of love for the family when Mephibosheth had nothing to offer him in return, and David adopted him as his own.

List five ways this story foreshadows Christ.

1)_____

_____

2)_____

_____

3)_____

_____

4)_____

_____

5)_____

_____

The New Testament offers another wonderful story about a great feast.

Read Luke 14:15–24.

What parallels do you see with Mephibosheth's story?_____

_____

_____

_____

_____

Jesus told this story of the banquet immediately after a man's statement about being blessed to be able to eat at the feast in the kingdom. Maybe this man believed, as most Jews did, that Jews were the only ones chosen by God to enter into the kingdom. If so, Jesus gave him an eye-opening new perspective.

Jesus told the story of a rich man who invited many people to a banquet. This was to be the party of the year. Anyone who was anyone would be there. But when the time came for the banquet, the invited guests offered ridiculously poor excuses for why they couldn't come. None of their excuses were logical. The guests made up reasons that should never have interfered with their ability to attend the banquet; they apparently didn't want to take the time to come.

Where did the man ask his servant to go to invite new people? _____

_____

_____

_____

_____

The incensed host ordered his servant to reach out to the marginalized ones of society: the poor, the crippled, the blind, and the lame (v. 21). He wanted them to take the seats the first invitees couldn't be bothered to fill. The servant said this had already been done but there was plenty of room for many more at the banquet table. Then the host, still wanting to have every available seat filled, ordered his servant to reach out further to the fringes of society, the ones way out in the country. He was most likely still referring to people with disabilities, the ones no one saw and everyone forgot.

What does this story say about the rejected, the socially marginalized, and the disabled? _____

_____

_____

_____

_____

That the invitation was extended to the disabled and the forgotten is very important. These were the types of people the Pharisees considered unclean and under judgment from God. Jesus taught that the kingdom was available not just to the Jews, the law-abiding "good guys", but it was even available to those regarded as unclean and disabled. Jesus explained God's grace to them in a way the audience would have understood. These people wouldn't have been willing to invite the disabled to their own dinner tables; they considered the disabled beneath them. But that is exactly what Jesus said God does. He cherishes the ones society forsakes. He personally calls them to eat at His table. He welcomes them to dine at His banquet. No matter how far away from the banquet they are, they are invited to take a seat and to partake of His generosity.

Here we see the unambiguous beauty of God's great grace. He invites every one of us to dine at His table. No matter our "defects", God showers His grace upon us all evenly. No one is worthless to God. We don't bring anything good to the banquet. We can't earn our way there. We can offer nothing to the King in return for His generosity. Just like Mephibosheth, while we are broken, while we are outsiders, we are adopted into the kingdom to dine with the King as His own. We are invited to the banquet just as we are. We only need to show up.

While the disabilities that others suffer mean that society might see them as less, it should remind us of our own brokenness, of our own weaknesses, and of our equal need for a place at God's table. What a sweet picture of the Lord's grace to save us all a spot at the table!

Read Luke 14:13–14.
"But when you give a banquet, invite the _____, the _____, the _____, the _____ and you will be blessed. Although they cannot repay you, you will be repaid at the resurrection of the righteous."

Read Matthew 25:40.
"The King will reply, 'I tell you the truth, whatever you did for one of the _____ of these brothers of mine, you did for me.'"

Cultures in the past and most certainly our culture today has taken an overarching negative view of people with disabilities. From misunderstanding how and why disabilities occur, to believing people with special needs are less than others or are a punishment from God, societies have tucked these people away, abandoning responsibility. But disabilities touch all social circles. From the wealthy to the poor, from country to country, disability has no bounds.

God has a purpose in the broken and the disabled. They are never forgotten.

Those of us with special needs children understand their worth. We understand their intrinsic value. We see beyond what the world sees to the precious child that is made in God's image. We face challenges in our role as parents and endure really difficult days, but our experiences enable us to bring something of value to society. We bring our own brokenness right along side our children's brokenness, and we show God's grace is for each one of us. We all get to sit at the same table together.

Group questions

Why does God allow weaker members in the body of Christ?_____

_____

Does knowing that God uses people with disabilities to fulfill His plans give you new insight into facing the situation with your child?_____

_____

_____

_____

Have you experienced something in your situation that you now see had a greater purpose than you initially thought?_____

_____

_____

_____

How can you or your child be an example of God's grace and mercy? _____

_____

_____

Week 4 notes

_____

_____

_____

_____

_____

_____

_____

_____

_____

Jen's Journal
January 16
I've been working on this post for a while, formulating my words and deciding what exactly I wanted to say. So here goes.

My son is not a punishment. God is not punishing me or my family for wrongs committed today or in the past. Liam is a joy to us. He's one of the greatest gifts we have ever received, and if he is supposed to be a punishment from God, well we just don't feel very penitent.

Liam's struggles and our struggles with his impairments do not make God less worthy of our praise and love. No matter how tough things get, we can always pull through and handle them with strength, knowing the Lord has placed us in this position for a purpose. And He trusts us to benefit from this and to be an encouragement to others who face trials and struggles. Do we like where He puts us? Heck no. It isn't easy and it isn't fun at times. God delights in making us uncomfortable because it's how we grow. It's hard being human, but we can endure the pain, knowing we serve an amazing God. We can get through the tough times, knowing there is purpose and peace at the end of the day.

Shawn and I have always joked about how God never guarantees us an easy life. This has made us look at the tough times in a different way. I've always said that the Lord doesn't owe me anything. My children are here because He decided to let me have them for a while. I had nothing to do with creating them, placing them in my womb, and growing them. I am not a god and cannot achieve creation on my own. The lives created are miracles of God's own doing. He knit them together. I have no idea why He would give me children in my womb but not let me raise them here on Earth. I don't understand it, but I trust that He is still a sovereign God who knows much more about how things should be run than I do. And at the end of my life, I will surely see how He laid everything out perfectly.

But for now, I will rejoice in our struggles us we journey through life. Liam has blessed our family in more ways than you can imagine. And at the end of the day, when I look at my precious little boy, I thank the Lord all over again for His mercy in allowing him to make it through the NICU. I thank the Lord for allowing Liam to come home so our family could get to know him, for giving him such a sweet personality that I can't help falling in love with him every day, and for giving me a chance to show the world what an awesome God we serve. He answers our prayers and grants His grace and mercy when we are so undeserving.

I know it might be hard for some to understand how I can thank God despite what we have been through. Giving thanks has been difficult when I have faced trials. I won't lie. I haven't enjoyed them. Our special needs journey has been really hard. I don't look at our trials and thank the Lord for what feels like unbearable pain and unspeakable loss. I am only human. But in the midst of my trials I still thank the Lord for what He has given me. There is always something to be thankful for because Jesus Christ took my punishment. Liam did not.

As the heavens
are higher than the
Earth, so are my ways
higher than your ways,
and my thoughts
than your thoughts.

Isaiah 55:9

Week 5
In the Image of God

By having the Holy Spirit inside us, we can spread the Kingdom of God wherever we go.

—Sunday Adelaja

Introduction

Most people will not know why they have a child with special needs. Those who do may not know why their child's disabilities exist to the extent they do. For instance, because my son was born so prematurely, he was at significant increased risk for various disabilities. Micro-preemies can have a wide range of special needs due to numerous circumstances that arise from leaving the womb so soon. We knew Liam was at risk for some problems. We knew he could face some special needs. But everyone was taken completely by surprise when the extent of his disabilities presented themselves and by how severely they affected his life. No one saw it coming. Even the doctors were shocked.

If you have adopted a child with special needs, you may not even be told much about your child's condition. You may get a few diagnostic labels but no specific details regarding your child's condition or the cause, leaving you with no real answers.

Some of you may have children who have special needs due to the sins of others. Babies born addicted to drugs or suffering from fetal alcohol disorders or shaken baby syndrome are victims of disabilities caused by others' poor judgment.

No matter what disabilities children suffer, no matter how they have arrived at their needs, no matter what they look like or what they can do, they have been made in the image of God. They were knit together in the womb and have been fearfully and wonderfully made. The secret of being human is never found in what we can offer others, it is found in the uniquely divine stamp of God within us all.

Lord, this week we pray that You will open our eyes to Your reality. Help us to see anew the value You bestow on us, and help us to remember that, no matter our condition, we are all made in Your image.

"Sons are a heritage from the Lord, children a reward from him" (Ps. 127:3–5).

Read Genesis 1:27.
"So God created man in his own image, in the _____ of _____ he created him; male and female he created them."

Theologians refer to this description of human beings as the *imago Dei*, translated from Latin as the "image of God."

What does it mean to be created in the image of God?_____
_____
_____

If you're like me, you might pause, unsure of what it actually means to be an image of God. How can we even truly describe God? Our words seem inadequate for description and yet we share His image? How can we possibly describe the awesome wonder of our heavenly Father?

If you research *imago Dei*, Theologians will provide several differing views on what the term means. How exactly could we be "god-like"? We may try to act like gods when it comes to running our own lives, pushing our agendas and thinking we've got everything under control, but we are clearly not God. We do not have God's attributes of sovereignty, providence, wisdom, goodness, or holiness, just to name a few. Leave us to our own devices and we will decidedly mess things up.

Animals are not made in the image of God even though he created them before us. He didn't put His imprint on them as He did on us. So what makes people the image bearers of God? What distinguishes us from all other created things? What makes us so special that God would put a bit of Himself in us?

God's image and ours have obvious dissimilarities and when we compare attributes we can find how we might be similar. God does not have a corporeal body, so we know that the human body is not what carries the entirety of the image of God. (Some theologians argue that the body does represent some aspects of God's image.) God is outside of time and space, so neither wisdom nor age makes us more like Him. So what attributes might we have that make us bear the image of God?

1) God has emotions:

"Anyone who does not_____ does not know God, because God is _____" (1 John 4:8).

"The one enthroned in heaven _____" (Ps. 2:4).

"Do not worship any other god, for the Lord, whose name is _____ is a _____ God" (Ex. 34:14).

"Then he rebukes them in his _____" (Ps. 2:5).

2) God is creative:

"In the beginning God _____ the heavens and the earth" (Gen. 1:1).

"Through him all things were _____; without him nothing was made that has been made" (John 1:3).

3) God is relational:

"God did this so that men would _____ him and perhaps reach out for him and find him; though he is not far from each one of us" (Acts 17:27).

4) God is spirit:

"God is_____ and his worshippers must worship in spirit and truth" (John 4:24).

5) God is righteous:

"For it is written: 'Be _____, because I am _____'" (1 Peter 1:16).

6) God is love:

"Whoever does _____ love does not _____ God, because God_____" (1 John 4:8).

What do you notice about these attributes?_____

_____

_____

While not an exhaustive list by any means, these are but a few of the verses found in the Bible that describe attributes of God that we share with Him. We can relate to these descriptions of His character at a very basic level. We feel a range of emotions, we are creative, we crave relationships, and we have eternal souls that will live on when our bodies are gone. And certainly not the least of all, we love. Oh, how we love and long to be loved! Being created in the image of God means that all humanity is worthy of honor and respect. There is nothing else like us in all of creation. We are sacred. No matter how they look or act, children with special needs are no different. They are created in the image of God, an image God finds so worthwhile, so valuable and honorable, that He forbids anyone from taking the life of another.

Read Genesis 9:6.

"Whoever sheds the _____ of man, by man shall his blood be shed; for in the _____ has God made man."

Read Exodus 20:13.

"You shall not _____."

Your child may not look or act like everyone else, but he or she still bears the same image of God that you and I do. My son is not capable of showing creativity: he cannot color, paint, or draw independently. Does this mean he doesn't bear the image of God? He cannot walk or talk; he cannot even roll over or sit by himself. Does this mean he is missing the image of God? Your child may not be able to have healthy relationships or to exhibit healthy emotions. Does he or she not carry the image of God?

According to God's Word, there is more to us than what the human body is capable of physically doing. Remember God's exchange with Moses from week 2? God took credit for creating people with body parts that don't function the way they were designed to do. That knowledge should give us great comfort because it means the functionality of the body is not what makes us and our children bearers of God's image. Each person has intrinsic value of inestimable worth that goes beyond what the body can do.

Read Luke 5:17–19.

"One day as he was teaching, Pharisees and teachers of the law, who had come from every village of Galilee and from Judea and Jerusalem, were sitting there. And the power of the Lord was present for him to heal the sick. Some men came carrying a paralytic on a mat and tried to take him into the house to lay him before Jesus. When they could not find a way to do this because of the crowd they went up on the roof and lowered him on his mat through the tiles into the middle of the crowd, right in front of Jesus."

As the mom of a child who cannot even hold his head up by himself, the account of this paralytic has always been very dear to my heart. I witness my son and his struggles to function in a body that doesn't work, and I get frustrated for him. As I read the story unfolding in Luke, I can imagine being there with them and I can relate to their situation. I understand their determination. I know I would have been just as desperate as these four men. I would have been willing to climb to the roof, make a hole, and lower my son down for an opportunity to be healed by the ultimate healer. Their love for the disabled man and their faith in the One who could heal him gave them the desire and the persistence they needed to place him right in front of Jesus. They went drastically and dangerously out of their way to get the man help.

Have you ever felt desperate enough to try something out of the ordinary to help your child? _____

_____

_____

Imagine the scene with me. In a house, many Pharisees and scribes are seated around Jesus. Back then the teachers sat and the students stood. So all the chairs are occupied by teachers of the law, wanting to hear from this new teacher, Jesus. The crowd of students is so large no one can get in the door. As men anxious to hear what Jesus has to say wait in this tightly packed room, they suddenly see a man being lowered on a mat through the roof down onto the floor. Can you imagine everyone's shock? The nerve of this man to interrupt their meeting and to expect to speak with Jesus. Does the room become silent as the men wait to see what Jesus will do? Do they become upset that this man has usurped them and has gotten an audience with the teacher? Can they see the desperation of this man and his friends, who have gone to such audacious extremes to get a face-to-face meeting with Jesus? Is Jesus amused at their tenacious spirit? Is Jesus impressed by their passion?

Read Luke 5:20.
"When Jesus saw their faith, he said, 'Friend, your sins are _____.'"

At first, Jesus did not deal with this man's noticeable physical condition. The man had an obvious disabling disorder. His friends went to great lengths to drop him through the ceiling to get him before Jesus for the opportunity to be healed. Clearly they believed Jesus could heal him of it. Having watched him dramatically lowered through the roof, everyone knew that's why this man was there. We can assume the man must want to receive physical healing, but Jesus doesn't even address his disability.

Jesus knew what this man really needed, and it wasn't anything physical or outwardly obvious. Jesus gave the man forgiveness. He pardoned his sins. Jesus went right to the heart of the man and said something that shocked the onlookers, because only God could forgive people of their sins. With this action Jesus taught us two significant points. First, we have a crucial need that goes beyond the physical realm; what's on the outside isn't the most pressing issue we face. Our greatest need is forgiveness of our sins. Second, Jesus showed He has the power to forgive sin.

What was the people's reaction to Jesus?_____

_____

Read Luke 5:21–26.

Jesus showed all those in the room that there is more to man's condition than meets the eye. While we may greatly desire to be made physically whole, what we actually need is spiritual wholeness. To prove to the people that He could offer the forgiveness He so freely gave the paralyzed man, Jesus completely healed him from his disabling condition.

We face brokenness in different ways than the paralytic did or our special needs children do, but we are all alike in our spiritual condition. We are all in need of forgiveness. We are not in perfect bodies with sinless natures, which means we all need to be made spiritually whole.

Read Romans 3:10–23.

"As it is written: There is no one _____ no not one."

As the mom of a severely disabled son, I find this verse can sting a bit. My sweet boy cannot sin like other children. He can't disobey me or talk back; he can't steal or lie or hurt me. He can't use his mouth to sling curses and spew bitterness (v. 14). His feet can't run swiftly toward sinful things (v. 15). It's hard to see him as sinful and unrighteous when he can't willingly sin; his body won't allow it. Yet, according to the Bible, he isn't righteous.

Does this verse bother you? Why or why not? _____

_____

Paul tells us there are no righteous people, meaning our precious children are not exempted. How can this be?

Read Romans 3:23.

"For _____ have sinned and fall short of the glory of God."

Read Psalm 51:5.

"Surely I was sinful at _____ sinful from the time my mother conceived me."

How is everyone sinful even at conception, even as a newborn baby? _____

_____

_____

Read Romans 5:12.

"Therefore, just as sin entered the world through one man, and death through sin, and in this way death came to all men because all sinned."

The unrighteousness we carry, the sin we all fall under, comes from the original sin of Adam and Eve in the Garden of Eden. Babies do not make a conscious decision to sin. Mentally handicapped teens and adults who function at a childlike level do not make a conscious decision to sin. But they, like all of us, suffer corruption from the fall and face the same punishment we all face; we all die because we have all been born into sin. Adam and Eve's punishment for their disobedience was death. Death entered into the futures of all men. Everyone dies, sometimes even the preborn, babies, and children. That is the curse. That is the judgment. Death comes for everyone because of corrupted human nature.

The fall and Old Testament law have condemned us. We face judgment. Paul wrote to the Corinthian church, "God made him who had no sin to be sin for us, so that in him we might become the righteousness of God" (2 Cor. 5:21). God used the law to set His people apart, bringing them closer to Him, while allowing the Law to show that we can never attain righteousness on our own. The law made our sins glaringly obvious and revealed how far from God we actually are.

Read Romans 6:23.

"The wages of sin is death, but the_____ of God is eternal life through Jesus Christ our Lord."

Read Romans 10:9–10.

"If you declare with your mouth, 'Jesus is Lord,' and believe in your heart that God raised him from the dead, you will be saved. For it is with your _____ that you believe and are justified, and it is with your _____ that you profess your faith and are saved."

Read Ephesians 2:8.

"For it is by _____ you have been saved, through _____and this is not from yourselves, it is the _____ of God."

Salvation from our sins comes through faith in Jesus Christ. We are made *imago Dei*, but as humans, we are incomplete. All of us are unrighteous and broken. We need Jesus. We need the forgiveness only He offers. We need the healing that comes only from facing our faults and from focusing on faith. Our need of salvation by faith in Christ alone reveals to us our inability to be self sufficient.

Can your child make a profession of faith in Jesus Christ? _____

_____

If not, do you ever worry because you don't know if your child has put trust for salvation in Jesus?

_____

_____

What does it mean for those of us who have severely handicapped children that cannot make a profession of faith in Jesus Christ? My son cannot speak. Understanding that Jesus died on the cross for our sins is not a concept he could understand. It's a scary thought to think God would send him to hell simply because he can't make a proper statement of faith. But does that sound like the God we see in the Bible? While the scriptures do not specifically discuss whether the mentally handicapped go to heaven, Jesus does makes a statement about children that can help shed some much-needed light on this topic for us.

Read Mark 10:13–16.

"People were bringing _____ to Jesus to have him touch them, but the disciples rebuked them. When Jesus saw this, he was _____. He said to them, 'Let the little children come to me, and do not _____ them, for the kingdom of God belongs to such as these. I tell you the truth, anyone who will not receive the kingdom of God like a little child will never enter it.' And he took the children in his arms and _____.''

We see Jesus doing several things here. First, He became indignant at His closest friends. Jesus respected these sweet little children and their faithful parents, and He got angry that the disciples had tried to prevent Him from spending time with them. Second, we see Jesus welcomed the children to Himself with open arms. He held them and blessed them.

In Jewish culture, it was customary for people to bring their little children before the elders of the synagogue for a blessing. The blessing would be a prayer over their lives; the elders would lay hands on the children and pray that God would pour out His goodness on them, that they would do good works and be faithful to God. We see numerous examples in the Old Testament of the patriarchal fathers blessing their children, so this was nothing new in Jewish culture and certainly nothing new for Jesus's disciples. It was customary for the faithful to have rabbis bless the children.

Caring parents brought their children to Jesus to have Him touch them and pray over them just like previous generations had done. It was a beautiful moment of God honoring faith for these families. But Jesus's closest friends got angry at the parents. Maybe the disciples thought Jesus's time was too valuable to waste on these little children. Or maybe they saw children as irrelevant to the task at hand: reaching people about the kingdom of God. Either way the disciples were wrong. Jesus became very angry with them. He actually gets irate at their attitude and told them they shouldn't prevent the children from coming to Him, "for the kingdom of God belongs to such as these."

Jesus valued spending time with these little children during his busy day, even the babies. They were important to Him. Did you catch the phrase *such as these?*

What do you think Jesus meant? _____

_____

_____

Jesus said the kingdom belongs to these little children, to babies, to infants—to people not old enough to make a faith statement. Jesus didn't put any rules on their membership in the kingdom before saying they belong. He didn't give their parents a litany of things to do first—circumcision, baptism, sacrificial offerings, religious rituals. Jesus matter-of-factly tells His disciples and anyone within earshot that babies and children are in the kingdom.

What does the kingdom of God mean?_____

_____

_____

Jesus was referring to the spiritual kingdom, His heavenly kingdom. He said children are in the kingdom. They belong. They don't have to profess their faith. In fact, they don't have to make a choice, because they *can't* make a choice. So then how are they allowed in the kingdom?

They are there entirely by God's grace! God gives special care and attention to His children who are not yet of an age to choose between good and evil, the ones who can't declare that they've put their faith in Jesus Christ. God's decision to impart salvation to those who cannot make a decision on their own shows His great love, protection, and care for the least in the kingdom.

The Pharisees, who held themselves superior in their knowledge of God and the law and in their devotion to following the law, would have found Jesus's statements to be unquestionably heretical. These children were incapable of doing good works, which was how the Pharisees believed people got themselves close to God. Jesus statement flies in the face of everything the Pharisees believed. Jesus said children enter the kingdom through God's sheer mercy and grace and they don't need to do anything good to get there. They don't have to earn their way in.

John Calvin said this: "Those little children have not yet any understanding to desire His blessing but when they are presented to Him, He gently and kindly receives them and dedicates them to the Father by a solemn act of blessing. It would be cruel to exclude that age from the grace of redemption. It is an irreligious audacity to drive from Christ's fold those whom He held in His arms and shut the door on them as strangers when He did not wish to forbid them."

Read Romans 1:18–23.

Paul says God has revealed Himself to all humanity since creation. People have no excuse for disbelief in Him. They know God exists, and yet they consciously choose to reject Him. How does this pertain to the mentally handicapped and to infants and children? Since babies and the mentally challenged are not aware of the general revelation of God in creation, they are excluded from being held accountable and facing judgment.

This fact should give all of us with severely disabled children great comfort and peace to our hearts. Those who cannot profess faith in Jesus, those who are not knowledgeable enough or who are too young to make a profession, are covered under the grace of our heavenly Father, and He imparts salvation to them. Jesus said they're in.

Read Deuteronomy 1:39.

"And the little ones that you said would be taken captive, your children who _____ yet know _____ from _____they will enter the land, I will give it to them and they will take possession of it."

This verse gives us another view of God's tenderness towards children. We read here that the children, too immature to understand the differences between good and evil, do not face the same punishment as those who can understand. There is accountability represented in this verse that implies children cannot be held culpable for their lack of knowledge.

Read 2 Samuel 12:13–23.

You are most likely familiar with this account of David and the death of his infant son. It's a tragic story of loss but also one of great hope. While his very ill baby boy was alive, David fasted and prayed for him. He wept over the boy, beseeching the Lord to save him. David refused to eat when his servants brought him food, and he would not get up from his prostrate position of prayer. He stayed that way for days and days, praying and hoping that God would let his infant son live. When the baby finally passed away, the servants were terrified to tell David the news. They saw how distraught he had been; what would he do now that his baby had died? How would he handle the devastating news? Upon learning of his son's death, David rose from the ground, bathed himself, worshiped the Lord, and then ate dinner. The servants were quite shocked at this change in his demeanor and confronted him about it. This was not the behavior they had expected. How could he behave this way all of a sudden?

How did David respond?_____

_____

What did David say he would get to do?_____

_____

Why do you think David had such a drastic shift in attitude? _____

_____

_____

David's attitude had completely changed. He'd done a one-eighty. He had thrown off his mantle of grief and had shaken off his despair. Why? How could he move on with his grief so suddenly? How could David be at peace so quickly? Could it be that David was certain his precious baby had entered into eternity with God? And he bore this confidence so greatly that when his beloved son died, he no longer grieved over him. David knew exactly where he had gone.

Read 2 Samuel 18:33.
What do you notice about David's grief in this verse? _____

_____

We see a marked difference between David's reaction to the death of his infant son and his reaction to the death of his other son, Absalom. David had a deep mournful, gut wrenching response to Absalom's death. He was heartbroken. His grief is almost palpable. After Absalom died, David wailed over and over, "O Absalom. O Absalom." His lamenting was so great it affected the morale of his men. David was horribly distraught upon Absalom's death. He didn't immediately rise, wash, and eat like before. He's in a state of mourning. Why such markedly different reactions from David to the deaths of his sons?

Absalom was a wicked and cruel man. He had raped his father's concubines, had his own brother killed, and conspired to usurp his father as king. Absalom was far removed from God and was full of corruption. Could David have reacted so differently to the two deaths because he knew he would see his infant son again but he would never see his evil son Absalom?

Did David's dramatically different reactions reflect his belief about where his sons would spend eternity?_____

_____

David knew he would be with his infant son again. He said as much. He said He would go where his son had gone. He no longer grieved over the boy once he had died for he knew they'd be together eventually. Yet for Absalom, David's sadness was completely overwhelming. His sorrow jumps off the pages and you can feel the depths of his grief. It's emotional to read his words and to feel his pain. Absalom was lost to him forever.

In *The Theology of Infant Salvation*, R. A. Webb says,

> If a dead infant were sent to hell on no other account than that of original sin, there would be a good reason to the divine mind for the judgment because sin is a reality, but the child's mind would be a perfect blank as to the reason of its suffering. Under such circumstances, it would know suffering but it would have no understanding of the reason for its suffering. It couldn't tell itself why it was so awfully smitten and consequently the whole meaning and significance of its sufferings being to it a conscious enigma, the very essence of the penalty would be absent and justice would be disappointed, cheated of its validation. Such an infant could feel that it was in hell, but it could not explain, to its own conscious, why it was there.

Do Jesus's words and the context in which we see David grieve help us reach a conclusion about the kingdom and children?_____

_____

Read Psalm 145:9.
"The Lord is good to all; he has _____ on all he has made."

Read 1 John 4:8.
"Whoever does not love does not know God, because God is _____."

The Lord God is good to all. He is full of tender compassion and shows mercy to all He has made. We can see God's tender loving care over His creation and over the most innocent of all, infants and children, who are created in His image. They are born under the curse just like all of us, but we hear in Jesus's words that the kingdom belongs to them. They cannot choose their salvation; they cannot choose to reject God and yet they will be in the kingdom. Would the God we read about in the Bible banish babies when they wouldn't even know why they were being punished? They receive no judgment, only God's tender mercy and compassionate grace. God in His infinite wisdom and sovereignty provides a place for them in the kingdom.

Read Mark 10:15.
"I tell you the truth, anyone who will not receive the kingdom of God like a _____ will never enter it."

What do you think Jesus is saying here?_____

_____

Jesus had just said in the previous verse that babies would have a place in the kingdom, and then He told these grown men that if they wanted to enter the kingdom they must become like children. I think that must have been an eye opening statement.

What attributes do babies and children have that most adults, in general, seem to lack?_____

_____

_____

When you think of children you might think of their innocence, trust, faith, simplicity, weakness, honesty, humility, or dependence. We outgrow a lot of these traits as we age. We no longer have the mind of a child. We no longer have that innocence. And yet Jesus said we must be like little children to enter the kingdom. Why? The kingdom is a gift freely given. We cannot achieve it by anything we do. We can't force our way in. We can't work our way in. Our security in the kingdom is achieved by humble and childlike faith alone. We are incapable of gaining the kingdom of God by ourselves.

Jesus's statement and David's recognition of his infant son's condition give great comfort to those of us who have lost a child.

Have you or someone close to you lost a child?_____

_____

Can you have full confidence about where children go after dying?_____

_____

Romans 1 along with the other passages we've studied this week point to a God of unending love and mercy. God, by His grace, reserves a place for innocent children in heaven. God loves us so much that He grants His mercy to those of us who have the knowledge to choose Him and also to those who cannot yet make that choice. We know that God does not want anyone to perish. "The Lord is not slow in keeping his promise, as some understand slowness. Instead he is patient with you, not wanting anyone to perish, but everyone to come to repentance" (2 Peter 3:9). Our heavenly Father wishes for everyone to be in His kingdom.

Our precious special needs children carry the same mark of God that all of us do. They are little missionaries in their own way; they help point people toward Jesus. We don't look at our children and immediately see the disabilities. We see a precious blessing. They carry with them innocence, humility, patience, openness, meekness, and love. They teach us to be thankful. Their lives carry hope and purpose and a promise that God loves every single one of us. Our children are *imago Dei*. With their challenges they remind us that we are all broken, all in need of saving. And God says nothing can separate us from His love other than our willful rejection of Him—not a disability, not pain or suffering, not even death.

> "No, in all these things we are more than conquerors through him who loved us. For I am convinced that neither death nor life, neither angels nor demons, neither the present nor the future, nor any powers, neither height nor depth, nor anything else in all creation will be able to separate us from the love of God that is in Christ Jesus our Lord" (Rom. 8:37–39).

Group questions
Have you ever considered how you and your child bear the image of God?_____
_____
_____

What attributes does your special needs child have that can point people toward God?_____
_____
_____

Have you ever pictured your special needs child as a missionary for God?_____
_____
_____

Week 5 notes
_____
_____
_____

_____

_____

_____

_____

_____

_____

_____

_____

Jen's Journal
May 11

I have a friend whose son died last month after a seizure only twelve days before he would have turned twenty years old. So young! His death was a complete surprise, totally unexpected. The family could not have prepared for it.

My friend lives in my old hometown, and I had been praying that I would get a chance to see her when we visited there recently. All I wanted to do was give her a hug—whether for me or for her, I don't know. I just know I wanted to tell her, in person, how sorry I was.

I had been standing in the lobby of our old church talking with friends, waiting for the right moment to join the service, which had already begun, when my friend walked out of the bathroom right in front of me. I looked at her, she looked at me, and then we hugged. We quietly cried in each other's embrace and let the tears flow. No words were needed. We were two mothers sharing tears of sadness over our losses, over each other's losses. Two mothers whose arms ached to hug the ones we missed. Two mothers joined by situations entirely different yet the same; we'd each lost a child too soon. She has memories to fall back on and misses the son she shared them with. I have no memories of times spent with my child and miss the opportunities I should have had.

My friend had a large bundle of tissues at the ready in her purse. We dabbed at our tears, and she asked me when it would get better. I don't know. I just know it gets easier.

It gets easier, but it never gets better. You are never better than you were before. You are marked by your loss. The loss of your child is forever with you. The slightest thought at the most random time can unleash a tidal wave of emotions that bring tears when you least expect them. Just when you think that you've shed your last tear, that you have gained the strength to move on without becoming emotional over the smallest thing, someone else's loss makes your loss become fresh and new again.

But we do have joy in these times through our faith in Christ.

We know God already knew how things were to be: "All the days ordained for me were written in your book before one of them came to be" (Ps. 139:16).

I don't know how people who have no hope in Christ deal with the loss of loved ones. How dismal and depressing to think that the only moments we have are here on earth and that once we die it's all over. There is no point, no future, no hope without Christ. Knowing we will see them again helps ease our sorrow. And while we have to learn to live this earthly life without our loved ones, we can have peace knowing that our loss is heaven's gain and that someday we will see them. That makes it easier.

Sons are a heritage from the Lord, children a reward from him.

Psalm 127:3

Week 6

Called to Serve

The only humility that is really ours is not that which we try to show before God in prayer, but that which we carry with us in our daily conduct.

—Andrew Murray

Introduction

Christian faith is uniquely and intrinsically bound up with service and servanthood. This week we will explore more of God's desire for us and how Jesus exemplified what it means to be a humble servant. As parents, we understand from the moment of our child's birth that we will be in service to that child for some time. We get a humbling crash course in serving someone else's needs first. The crying baby won't wait for you to finish your meal. Sometimes you won't even get the meal. From the start, our kids will need us to care for all of their daily needs before anyone else's. Over time they should become productive, independent adults, and the demands to meet all their needs will have long since faded. But some of us special needs parents will never see the day when we are not in service to our children. Some of us may have children who will never lead independent lives.

Your child may struggle to walk; your son with oppositional defiant disorder may exhibit violent outbursts; your child with autism may not be able to express themselves well; your daughter may suffer pain from seizures or contractures from cerebral palsy. However, our children do not face these issues on their own. We fight right along side them in their battles by guiding, serving, and supporting them in every way possible.

God takes great delight in our willingness to serve the needs of our special needs children. There is something inherently beautiful found in our service to others. The greatest example of servanthood that we can look to is found in Jesus Christ. In service to God, He willingly gave up His life for us.

While He was here He gave us definitive examples of what being a servant looks like. These examples are to help us keep the right focus when we regularly deal with difficult circumstances.

Lord, this week help us to understand more clearly how You view service and having a servant's heart, not only with our children but toward others as well.

"Bear one another's burdens and thereby fulfill the law of Christ" (Gal. 6:2).

Is there a difference between slave and servant?_____
_____

People tend to confuse servant with the modern day notion of slavery. Most of the slavery seen in the Old Testament was actually servanthood, or voluntary slavery. People would sell themselves into indentured servitude and have their debts discharged after a set period of time. Back then there was no government for the people to fall back on in extremely difficult times. There were no food stamps, unemployment checks, or local soup kitchens. In situations such as these, people could choose servitude instead of suffering starvation and homelessness. They would be well taken care of while they worked. They would receive food, housing, and clothing. They would eventually be freed from their obligations after years of service. God did not intend for people to keep slaves. In fact, God made a law against it (Ex. 21:16) along with other laws to protect slaves from harm.

Read Deuteronomy 15:12–17.
The Indentured Servant
When was the servant allowed to go free? _____

What three things was the servant required to receive when his time was up?_____
_____

God does not want anyone taking advantage of His people. If someone had to sell themselves into servitude and their time of service was up, God did not expect them to walk away empty-handed after all their years of hard work. A day's provisions weren't even enough to send them on their way; God said the owner was to supply provisions *liberally* from his personal flock, his threshing floor, and his winepress. God made sure servants would be leaving with enough supplies to help them get back on their feet. They were to go on their way fully supplied with livestock, food, and drink. This would be somewhat of a cost to the owner but would assure the servants had a healthy start in their new independence. They couldn't get started on their new life without help, and God made sure they got plenty of it.

Read Exodus 21:5–6.

The Loyal Servant

"But if the servant declares, 'I love my master and my wife and children and do not want to go free,' then his master must take him before the judges. He shall take him to the door or the doorpost and pierce his ear with an awl. Then he will be his servant for life."

Do you see any connection between the servant and our servanthood in Christ?_____

_____

_____

_____

Is there a difference between servitude and servanthood?_____

_____

_____

_____

If a servant developed a healthy and positive relationship with their master, they could choose to stay under their leadership and guidance indefinitely. In this case, they would be making a lifetime commitment to serve, giving up their rights permanently to the master. The servant's decision to remain with his master wouldn't be kept a secret. The act would take place in a public ceremony at which a sharp tool was used to pierce a hole in the servant's ear, signifying lifetime obedience in servanthood to the master. This decision was immutable. There was no going back. Once the servant had his ear pierced, he would always be branded as a bond servant. This was an outward mark of his new identity that he would wear proudly, signifying he was not his own.

There are some fascinating correlations between the piercing of the servant's ear on the doorpost, believers surrendering themselves to Jesus Christ, and Jesus surrendering of Himself to the Master's will.

Jesus said several times in John 10 that he was the gate or door. Jesus was a humble servant, who was pierced on the cross, and was forever marked for His submission to God. His life was not His own; Jesus did as God commanded.

Servant, pierced, proud to be forever marked for the master—that's us too! Isn't it just like God to weave a string through the Old Testament with hints of Jesus and our relationship to Him? We are free to choose whether or not we want to be proudly marked for life in service to Him, just like the loyal servant in Exodus.

Many Hebrew patriarchs and leaders in the Old Testament were referred to as servants. Who is mentioned in the verses below?

Genesis 26:24_____

Numbers 12:7_____

Joshua 24:29_____

2 Samuel 7:5_____

Isaiah 20:3_____

Isaiah 53:11_____

Jeremiah 7:25_____

Does the word *servant* have a positive or negative connotation for you?_____

_____

What do you think God's criteria are in His choice of servants?_____

_____

_____

Read Exodus 14:31.
"And when the Israelites saw the mighty hand of the Lord displayed against the Egyptians, the people feared the Lord and put their trust in him and in Moses his _____."

Read Deuteronomy 34:5.
"And Moses_____ died there in Moab, as the Lord had said."

Read 2 Samuel 7:8.
"Now then, tell _____ David, 'This is what the Lord Almighty says: I took you from the pasture, from tending the flock, and appointed you ruler over my people Israel.'"

Do these verses paint a negative portrait of being a servant?_____

_____

What characteristics do we need to be a servant?_____

_____

One of the main factors in God's choosing of His servants is the heart. Wealth, position, birth order, talent, appearance, and education don't seem to count much for consideration. Praise God! Having the heart of a servant has more to do with your relationship with God than anything else. Your willingness to allow yourself to be used for His glory shows others the desire of your heart: following after God. Nothing more beautifully expresses your faith in God than your willingness to serve Him in the capacity to which He calls you. When you see a need and you meet it, when you move beyond your comfort zone to help others, when you humble yourself and put others' needs before yours, you show others that Christ lives in your heart.

Read Ephesians 3:17.

"So that Christ may dwell in your _____ through faith."

The prophetic Old Testament books of Isaiah and Zechariah portray Christ as a humble servant to come. Jesus proudly called Himself a servant and served God and people in the deepest sense of the word. This shows us that servanthood should not be viewed in a disparaging light. Our view of Jesus and how He served others isn't a negative one. Why, then, should we view serving others as such a burden? Why is it so hard to see service as noble, honorable, and worth the effort?

Read Mark 10:45.

"For even the Son of Man did not come to be served, but to _____ and to give his _____ as a ransom for many."

Read Ephesians 2:10.

"For we are God's workmanship, created in Christ Jesus to do _____ works, which God prepared in advance for us to do."

Read John 13:4–17.

The Humble Servant

What stands out for you in this passage? _____

_____

_____

In the first century, when you walked on the dusty dry ground, your feet would become covered in dirt. Large amounts of cattle and horse droppings would add to the filthiness on the roads. Your feet would become so dirty that you would need to wash them before dining or getting into bed. Whenever guests were invited into a home, the servant or otherwise lowliest member of the household would wash the guests' feet before dinner. When dining back then, you would recline at the table to eat your meal, so filthy feet would be near each guest, the table, and the food. It was common hospitality to have your feet washed.

What example of servanthood do we see in Jesus's actions?_____

_____

Jesus and the disciples were meeting privately in the upper room of the home. There were no servants to remove their shoes or to wash their feet for them before the meal. No one thought to take this task upon himself, but Jesus unselfishly did so. The disciples were probably stunned. This was such a lowly, menial task. Peter, to his credit, was the only one to protest this action. Peter was shocked that their teacher would do something so beneath Him. He didn't want Jesus to wash his feet, but Jesus said if Peter wouldn't allow Him to do it, then he didn't know Jesus. Peter's reaction toward Jesus prevented him from seeing what Jesus was really doing.

What did Jesus mean when he said, "Unless I wash you, you have no part with me"?_____

_____

_____

When Jesus finished His task, He asked the disciples if they understood what He had just done. Jesus was teaching them a lesson about humility; how to be humble in honor of and in service to God. It was not beneath Jesus to serve others, and it should not be beneath us to serve each other. If He could wash filthy feet, we can wash filthy feet. If we want to participate in a life with Jesus, we must be willing to perform the lowliest of tasks. If Jesus Christ was willing to humbly and unconditionally serve His followers in such a lowly way, elevating others over Himself, we should follow His example. We should be willing to perform even the most disagreeable tasks for others in obedience to Christ.

The disciples didn't see it then, but they would eventually understand that Jesus's act of washing their feet showed them how to be humble in service to God and His people.

What can we learn from Jesus's humility?_____

_____

What did Jesus say will happen when we serve?_____

_____

Have you ever taken part in a foot washing ceremony?_____

_____

Some years ago at one of our special needs camps in Belarus, we were creating T-shirts, using the kids' footprints to make angels. We wanted the children to have a fun memento of their week in camp that would be unique to each one. We took their sweaty, unwashed in days, filthy feet and coated them with ink, stamping them onto the shirts, grime and all. Holding their dirty feet immediately reminded me of Jesus's words in John 13. I am not a fan of feet let alone dirty feet, and I felt a little ashamed. Jesus could wash feet. Couldn't I stamp feet? I decided to be grateful for the opportunity to go outside of my comfort zone, by focusing on the beauty God sees when we serve. God has so much to teach us about humility when we allow Him to turn our world upside down. I believe I gained more out of that moment than the children did.

Read Luke 12:41–48.
The Abusive Servant
What is the servant to be found doing when the master returns? _____
_____

What are the expectations of the ones who have been entrusted with much? _____
_____

In this parable Jesus emphasized that those given positions of authority over others have a responsibility to serve. And in typical Jesus fashion, this parable can have several meanings, all of which are relevant and on point. Jesus was an amazing storyteller, and His parables are still important and relatable, hitting at the heart of issues we face today.

In light of your experiences with your child with special needs, what meaning does this parable have for you when you consider those who might abuse or take advantage of those with special needs?__
_____
_____

We should take comfort in knowing that these people will eventually face the consequences of their behavior. The key line in this section is in verse 48: "From everyone who has been given much, much will be demanded; and from the one who has been entrusted with much, much more will be asked." God has entrusted us to be servants of our children, and we are to be found serving them well when the Master returns. Those who do not take the privilege of this responsibility seriously will be held accountable. God has entrusted us with children who have specific needs. He has given much responsibility to us. God does not seek perfection from us as we serve our children. He seeks our hearts.

Read Matthew 25:14–30.
The Irresponsible Servant

What is your initial reaction to the man who buried his talent? _____

_____

Do you find the servant's punishment harsh? _____

_____

In this parable we see the master trusting his servants with talents. A talent was a very large sum of money. Some estimate one talent was worth more than $1,000; others argue it was worth significantly more. Either way a talent was very valuable and we read that the master trusted each servant with differing amounts. Why would he do this? While this may seem unfair at first, we see that in the end, each servant received exactly what he was capable of reproducing. The effort they put forth was what they received back in the end.

Our modern-day use of the word *talent* is derived from this parable. Knowing that the talents in the story were to be invested and grown, what talents do you have that you can invest and grow as a servant to Jesus?_____

_____

_____

The servant entrusted with only one talent buried his. He did not grow it or attempt to work with it in any way. He hid it away in fear, and while nothing bad happened to it, nothing good came from it either. He was punished for doing nothing with his talent.

How does this parable relate to having a child with special needs? _____

_____

_____

There is an application of this parable that applies to our situation as special needs parents. We have been entrusted with a huge responsibility that we shouldn't take lightly. Our kids depend on us to nurture them, to help them grow, and to reach new heights. The job we face as parents looks nothing like the job other parents face. Remember, those parents may have been entrusted with less "talents" than you. Your parenting will be unique to you and unique to your child because that is the *talent*, the opportunity, God entrusted specifically to you. He trusts you to work with and to enrich what you've been given.

Read 1 Peter 4:10–11.

"Each of you should use whatever gift you have received to _____ others, as faithful stewards of God's grace in its various forms_____ so that in all things God may be praised through Jesus Christ."

Have you gained new "talents" as you've traveled on your special needs journey with your child? ___

_____

_____

Read John 15:20.

"Remember the words I spoke to you; _____ servant is greater than his master."

Read Matthew 10:24.

"A student is _____ above his teacher, nor a servant above his master."

Read Luke 22:27.

"For who is _____, the one who is at the table or the one who _____? Is it not the one who is at the table? But I am among you as _____."

How did Jesus describe Himself in Luke 22:27? _____

What does it mean to have the heart of a servant?_____

_____

Jesus put every person on equal ground. Everyone is important and valuable; status, abilities, and disabilities do not matter. Greatness in the kingdom of God is never found in positions or titles. A servant is not greater than his master. We may automatically think the master is above the servant because of their positions but Jesus said that while the master and the servant may have very different roles and responsibilities, they are actually equals. No one is better than another. He repeated this concept numerous times in the Gospels and demonstrated that service to others is honorable, humbling, and important. Service to others builds our character, maturing us and growing us as we walk with Christ. Having a servant's heart aligns our attitude with Jesus.

Read Philippians 2:3–5.

"Do nothing out of selfish ambition or vain conceit, but in humility consider others better than yourselves. Each of you should look not only to your own interests, but also to the interests of others. Your attitude should be the same as that of Christ Jesus."

Read Ephesians 6:7.

"Rendering service with a good will as to the Lord and not to man."

Read Colossians 3:23.

"Whatever you do, work heartily, as for the Lord and not for men."

What does it mean to have the heart of a servant?_____
_____

Read Matthew 20:20–28.

"Jesus called them together and said, 'You know that the rulers of the Gentiles lord it over them, and their high officials exercise authority over them. Not so with you. Instead, whoever wants to become great among you must be your servant, and whoever wants to be first must be your slave—just as the Son of Man did not come to be served, but to serve, and to give his life as a ransom for many.'"

Why is God's standard of servanthood so important?_____
_____
_____

Is being a servant easy?_____
_____

Do you think society today sees this as something positive or negative?_____
_____
_____

I know we can sometimes feel like we are slaves to our children, not because they are masters over us but because we work hard for them and always have to put their needs first. Our lives are no longer our own. We are no longer in control. Our course is determined by our children and their needs. Their lives demand our all. And when we give all we've got, when we feel there is very little left of the person we used to be, when we are exhausted from one more soul-aching day, and still the needs of our children demand more, we can feel like we have become their slaves.

While we are not slaves to our children with special needs, we are without a doubt in service to them. However, there is someone whom we can be called a slave to, and that is Jesus Christ. This is not a popular way to describe our relationship to Jesus, but if we take the words of the New Testament in their proper context, we cannot fail to see this remarkable aspect of our relationship to Him.

The Greek word for slave, *doulos*, is used more than a hundred times in the New Testament and specifically in reference to followers of Jesus. *Doulos* means to "bind" a person to someone else. This person would lose his autonomy, his freedom, his independence. He was no longer his own, just like the loyal servant in Exodus 21. The term *doulos*, or slave, was a favorite description of the apostles themselves for their relationship to Jesus. Paul used it in almost all of his letters. Even James, Jesus's oldest brother, who didn't believe in who Jesus was at first, called himself *doulos*, a slave to Jesus.

Read James 1:1.

"James, a _____ of God and of the Lord Jesus Christ."

What a turning point in the life of this brother of Jesus to go from an adamant unbeliever to willingly calling himself a slave! James's use of the word *slave* underscores his humility in exclusive service to his own brother. He was calling his brother his master. Because context is always essential in the Bible, it's important to look at the culture during the time of these writings. The word *doulos* meant slave, not servant. There were six different variations of the Greek word for "servant," and *doulos* was never one of them. It always meant "slave." Because of the awful connotations of the word *slave*, the word *doulos* has been translated as "servant" in nearly all Bible versions today. But to understand the full implications of what Paul and James were saying to the recipients of their letters, we must understand the true meaning of the word *doulos*. They didn't use this word lightly. The word *slave* had very negative connotations in their society just as it does in ours today. They lived in a time of rampant, abusive slavery, and in spite of this, they felt their relationship with Jesus was best described by using the term for slave.

In the Greco-Roman culture, *doulos* referred to the lowest class of society. These were the people with no rights, no privileges, no independence, and certainly no freedoms. They were to do their master's bidding at all times and were seen as expendable. Paul and James are implying that they view themselves as bound totally and completely to Jesus just like a slave is to his master. Out of love and devotion, they have willingly surrendered their lives in full service to Him. They belong to Jesus.

Read Romans 1:1.

"Paul, a _____ of Jesus Christ, called to be an apostle, set apart for the gospel of God."

Remember, in the original Greek, the word used here is actually *doulos*. Paul uses the word *slave*. What a description Paul gives of himself; he's a slave of Jesus. His life is no longer his own. He is no longer in control. He is no longer independent and free to do as he wishes. He belongs to someone else. The people of his time knew exactly what he meant when he used the word *doulos*.

Read Matthew 6:24.

"No one can _____ two _____. Either he will hate the one and love the other or he will be _____ to the one and _____ the other."

Matthew 6:24, translated from Greek, says, "No man can be a slave to two masters." Your Bible probably says, "No man can serve two masters." But Jesus used the word *doulos*. Jesus was saying it is impossible to be a slave to two masters. We can belong to only one master. We can have only one owner. Who will your master be?

Read 1 Corinthians 7:23.

"You were bought at a price; do not become slaves of men."

Read Colossians 3:24.

"Since you know that you will receive an inheritance from the Lord as a reward. It is the Lord Christ you are _____."

The NIV translation says "serving." But again, Paul uses the word *doulos* here, and the line is more appropriately translated as "It is the Lord Christ to whom you are *enslaved*." Because of our choice to be slaves to Christ, to be permanently bound to Him, we are to honor Christ. We should want to live our lives in happy obedience, serving God, not the world and not ourselves.

Understanding the meaning of *doulos*, can you say you are a slave to Jesus Christ? _____

_____

Being a slave to Jesus Christ is beyond comparison because our Master makes us His sons and daughters, adopting us into His family, treating us as His own. He provides for us and cares for us. We are invited to dine at His banquet forever. Why wouldn't we want to be bound to Him as slaves? We will be slaves to someone or something whether we realize it or not. What a joy and a privilege we have in choosing to be a slave of Jesus Christ!

Your service to your children with special needs will speak volumes to everyone around you as you willingly support, encourage, and care for them. You never know who is watching you and your family. I have been amazed over the years at the people who have thanked me for the example of living my life for God's kingdom in spite of my daily struggles with a severely handicapped child. I am always shocked when someone makes a comment, because I have never felt like I'm an example for anything. I miss my old life. This journey has been very hard, without a doubt, and I've done my fair share of complaining in the trenches, but to know that people still see Jesus shine through in my struggles inspires me. My prayer is that I am serving my children well as a slave to Jesus.

Not everyone handles difficult situations with a praiseworthy attitude. Not everyone who receives a special needs child views this as a blessing. Not everyone who has a child born with special needs is capable of loving, caring for, or serving such a child. We need to give the situation over to God with an attitude of praise, believing that when we have a servant's heart, our circumstances will bring us and those around us closer to God. We can be a light in the dark for those who feel overwhelmed in the storm. God has a purpose. We can pray, we can love, and we can serve.

When we see Christ, we see service. Jesus gave us an example of how to serve. He commanded that we do the same, and He lived His life in demonstration of that. Why we serve and how we serve matters because whom we serve matters. We are to be slaves to Christ.

Group questions

What does it mean to be a slave of Jesus Christ?_____

_____

_____

Do you feel like you are a slave to your child? _____

_____

_____

Do you ever feel like you are serving the Lord by serving your child?_____

_____

_____

Are you willing to be a servant with the call God has given you for your life?_____

_____

_____

Week 6 notes

_____

_____

_____

_____

_____

_____

_____

_____

_____

_____

Jen's Journal

April 21

I always tell my kids that if anyone ever questions them about God's existence, they should have them speak to me and I could surely show the skeptic how real God is in my life. Whether they chose to follow Him or not is entirely up to them, but God is clearly alive and working in me. There are too many stories, too many coincidences, too many unspoken answered requests for me to deny that my Savior lives and is actively involved in my life.

Last year when my two oldest kids were heading off on a mission trip to Costa Rica, I told Shawn I wanted to go with them the next year because they were working with kids in orphanages and my heart has always desired to help orphans in some way. Our church was also sending a team to Belarus (a former Soviet Union republic) to run a Bible camp for special needs kids and their families. Both teams were at the church that day, being prayed over before they all shipped out. Shawn asked me why I wouldn't prefer to go to Belarus since I was heavily involved in the special needs area with our son and with our church. He thought that would be a better fit. I told him it wasn't my thing. I was already actively involved and working with special needs kids. I didn't need to travel halfway around the world to do more of that.

Three days later, I was driving Liam to therapy, praying over my kids and their team in Costa Rica. Suddenly my prayers were interrupted and I heard, "You're going to Belarus next year." Out of the blue, clear as day, I heard I was going to Belarus next year. Excuse me? What?

You have to understand that I had no desire to go to Belarus. None. The possibility had never crossed my mind, and I had discussed the subject only because Shawn brought it up. It wasn't my thing. Yet there I was in prayer over my children when a word from God came out of the blue. It was bizarre.

At first I wondered whether my crazy brain wasn't playing tricks on me, but when I realized that I wasn't even praying for the Belarus team and that I didn't want to go there, I knew this was absolutely a word from God. I got the chills. I was scared and I said nothing to anyone.

The team got back two weeks later. One of the members got off the plane, went home, and immediately called me. He told me, "You're going to Belarus next year." Uh, what?

I was floored. I wish he could have seen the shock on my face. I made excuses: It's too expensive. I just don't know. I'd have to think about it. And then he said, "No, really, you are going next year. God already told me."

I didn't tell him right then what I had clearly heard God say to me in prayer two weeks earlier. I kept it quiet until I saw his wife, and still in a state of unbelief, I shared with her what had happened. I told her the whole story. She pointed out that the plan had been confirmed to me three different times over three weeks. It was pretty hard to dispute that I should go. God was calling me to serve.

God has had my back every step of the way. All of the money needed to get my team over to Belarus has been raised. God has worked out all the plans, and everything is going perfectly for our team to live courageously, answering His call to serve and to work with special needs families and their children.

How amazing is our God? I freely admit I had no desire to go, but God has seen fit to send me and I couldn't be more excited now. I know this trip is for His glory and will serve a huge purpose not only in my life but in the lives of all those who will hear the story. I am proof that we have an active God who speaks and wants us to say yes.

Carry eachothers burdens & in this way you will fulfill the law of Christ.

Galatians 6:2

Week 7

Hope, Trust, and Peace for the Journey

> If you have been reduced to God being your only hope, you are in a good place.
>
> —Jim Laffoon

Introduction

What is your heart full of? Is it full of hope? Is it full of expectations of greater things to come? Do you hope for a better tomorrow with a better house, a better car, a better job? Or do you hope just to make it through one more day? Do you hope today doesn't end in a mental breakdown for you or your special needs child? Do you hope there is hope for your child? Do you have one of your hopes dashed only to replace it with a new hope? And what happens when that hope is dashed? Do you give up hope entirely?

Misplaced hopes can be devastating. There is nothing wrong with having hopes as long as they don't interfere with God's desires for your life. We live in a home purchased right before our special needs son was born. It is not a wheelchair-friendly residence; in fact, it is completely wheelchair- unfriendly. There is only one bedroom downstairs, the master, and Liam has to sleep in our room for many reasons. He sleeps on a toddler mattress on the floor to keep him safe when he falls off of the bed. I could not fathom the reason God would let us buy this home and less than a year later have a child with so many disabilities that the home doesn't work for us at all. I have a lot of questions about this part of our journey. Do I hope someday to have a home where we can freely maneuver my son's wheelchair through the house, be able to take him into the bathroom, to bathe him properly, and give him his own bedroom? Absolutely! But I have learned to be at peace with this house. It isn't an accident that we are here, and I trust that God knows what He's doing even when it makes no sense to me. My hope is in Him, not in my circumstances.

We have so many hopes for our special children. And that's a wonderful thing! Hope helps guide us. It keeps us fighting for the next best thing for our kids. It keeps us working hard to help them reach goals. It helps us seek better opportunities and better care to help them achieve more of their potential. Hope helps us get up in the morning. Our day-to-day struggles will be isolating, frustrating, and overwhelming. But if we aren't putting our hope in the right place, we will become more isolated, frustrated, and overwhelmed. Hope cannot be found in the things of this world. This world will fail us at every turn. When we feel like we can't get through another day, when the hurts have piled up and become too much, we need to draw on the hope found in God's Word.

Hope and trust are synonymous and can be used interchangeably. God says He can be trusted. And when we fully embrace this knowledge, when we fully hope in Him, He will give us peace. Hope will heal our hurts.

Father, we know it pleases You when we put our hope in You alone. Help us to lean on You and to draw our strength from You. Please give us peace that surpasses all understanding when things don't make sense. Help us to remember our circumstances don't define us—You do.

> "Guide me in your truth and teach me, for you are God my Savior, and my hope is in you all day long" (Ps. 25:5).

Read Isaiah 40:29–31.
"He gives _____ to the weary and increases the power of the weak. Even youths grow tired and weary, and young men stumble and fall; but those who _____ in the Lord will _____ their strength. They will soar on wings like eagles, they will run and not grow weary, they will walk and not be faint."

What does Isaiah say God does for the weary?_____

_____

What can we do to renew our energy and strength?_____

_____

While this section of scripture was addressed to the Israelites living in Babylon, it has meaning for us today. We see an encouraging attribute of God: His strength. He never tires, giving us all the support we need in our weaknesses. Isaiah contrasts God's inexhaustible strength with the power and might of young men. Think of the energy young boys have. They can go all day long, running from one activity to the next, racing around with boundless energy, but eventually even they will wear out and become tired. Little boys can't go on forever without recharging at some point. Not so with God. He never becomes exhausted. His power is endless. Doesn't scripture give us a beautiful picture of His abilities here? As the parent of a child with special needs, I would paraphrase the passage this way: He gives strength to the special needs mom and increases her capabilities. Even though she may be tired and stumble after another sleepless night, when she puts her hope in the Lord, He will be her strength.

Amen and amen! The Lord is our strength! Now contrast this passage with what Paul says in 2 Corinthians 12:9: "But he said to me, 'My grace is sufficient for you, for my power is made perfect in weakness.'" Again we see the parallel of the strength of the Lord displayed in us when we are weak and weary. We special needs parents often feel weak and weary. At least I do. The physical and mental demands of dealing with a nonambulatory kid wear me out. I know we all face different challenges that are demanding in their own right. We have so much on our plates, and trying to balance everything all at once is exhausting. We've all looked to God and wondered if He sees everything we are trying to carry. To know that God will strengthen us on those dark days when things seem to be crashing all around us should give us immense hope! He will renew and strengthen us when we put our hope in Him.

Read Psalm 147:11.

"The Lord delights in those who fear Him, who put their _____ in his unfailing _____."

Why do you think God is delighted when you put your hope in Him?_____
_____

God wants you to know you can trust Him. He wants you to know it with every fiber of your being. You can put all of your hope in Him because He is trustworthy. He delights in His children just like you take delight in your children. You want your children to know you can be trusted to provide support and comfort in times of trouble. You want your children to come running to you when something goes wrong and they need reassurance. You want to be their soft place to land. God is the same. He desires that we come to Him in our pain and fear; He wants us to run to Him just a like child would run to their parent. He is our Father and He wants to comfort us when we are hurting.

Read Psalm 33:18, 20–22.

"But the eyes of the Lord are on those who fear him, on those whose _____ is in his unfailing _____. We wait in hope for the Lord; he is our _____ and our _____. In him our hearts rejoice, for we trust in his holy name. May your unfailing _____ be with us, Lord, even as we put our _____ in you."

What does this psalm say we are to do in our hope?_____

_____

What does it say the Lord does for us? _____

What do we receive when we put our hope in the Lord?_____

Think about the purpose of a shield. Have you ever ridden a motorcycle without wearing a helmet that has a face shield? It's pretty painful to have a bug hit you in the face when you are traveling at a high speed. You've probably experienced a rock hitting the windshield of your car. Can you imagine your car without the windshield and the dangers you'd be in if it wasn't there? Those shields are intended to protect you from danger. Their purpose is to prevent you from experiencing pain and harm.

The word *shield* also means to guard and to defend. In battle, a soldier will hold his shield up to protect his body from deadly blows. It's his primary protection against the enemy. It's his first line of defense. Not just as Christians but also in our walk as special needs parents, we will be bombarded by attacks from the Enemy, seeking to wear us down and to get us to put down our shields. On our journey we will eventually end up walking very near to the Enemy. Our first line of defense is to keep God as our shield to protect us from the blows that will inevitably come our way.

Psalm 30:20–22.

"We wait in hope for the Lord; he is our help and our _____. In him our hearts rejoice, for we trust in his holy name. May your unfailing love be with us, Lord, even as we put our _____ in you."

The word *trust* and its synonym, *hope*, are frequently used in the Bible. The Old and New Testaments often speak of where we are to put our faith. God does not leave us hopeless. We cannot predict what life will look like for us down the road with our special needs children. But, we can be sure that God delights in us and in them and that we are loved and cherished by a heavenly Father who does not leave us for a second.

Read Jeremiah 17:7–8.
"But blessed is the one who _____ in the Lord, whose confidence is in him. They will be like a tree planted by the water that sends out its roots by the stream. It does not fear when heat comes; its leaves are always green. It has no _____ in a year of drought and never fails to bear fruit."

What happens to a tree if its roots don't stretch down deep enough to get the nourishing water from the bedrock? The shallow roots, while providing enough water to sustain the tree, will not be strong enough to hold the tree in place when the strong storms come. The tree will not be able to withstand the pressure, and the many shallow roots will give way, allowing the tree to topple over.

That can happen to us if we aren't planting the truth deep within ourselves for proper and necessary growth. When we are rooted in trust that God is for us and not against us, when we plant knowledge of His Word deep into our hearts, our hope and faith will grow strong. We will not fear when the unavoidable storms of life come our way, because they will not be able to sway us from our deeply rooted faith. We will have the strength to stay strong and grow tall, branching out and reaching others with the hope we have been given. When our hope and trust are securely rooted and are nourished with God's Word, we will bear fruit in the lives of our family members, friends, coworkers, and even strangers.

Do you feel you have been able to bear fruit where God has planted you?_____
_____

Do you feel you are rooted deeply enough in God's Word to hold strong when the storms come?___
_____

In what areas of your life do you still need to surrender to God? _____
_____
_____

Read Psalm 71.

King David is believed to have written this psalm in his old age when he had years of wisdom from which to draw upon. If you write or highlight in your Bible, this is a great place to do that. This psalm is full of hope, remembrances of God's intervention in David's life, and praises for what He had done. David's life wasn't always easy and yet he always held his hope in God. It's a beautiful psalm to turn to when we are struggling.

How long did David have hope in the Lord?_____
_____

What does *portent* mean (v. 7)?_____
_____

Was David using the word *portent* in a positive or negative way?_____
_____

In the next verse David praises God. He expresses his hope in God throughout the psalm.

Why do you think David was so full of hope?_____
_____
_____

David had a lifetime of experience with God to reflect on and to draw strength from when times got tough. David remembered God's acts in his life over many decades, recalling His marvelous deeds (v. 17). He drew from those memories of God's care for him to continue to have hope even when others said God had forsaken him (v. 11). David could not believe God would ever leave him, because he had a history with God that went beyond what he was feeling in the current moment. He could draw on that history in times of doubt.

Do you have memories of God or of His actions in your life that you can recall when you start to feel distant from Him? _____

If you are a new Christian you may not have many personal experiences to recall when times are tough. That's ok! If you're new to Him, remember that He isn't new to you. God has been behind the scenes of your story all along. Go to His Word and recall what He's done for others, like David, and take refuge in His promises.

When we put our hope in the right source we can experience knowledge and peace that set us free.

Read Jeremiah 29:11–13.
"For I know the _____I have for you," declares the Lord, "plans to _____
you and not to _____ you, plans to give you _____ and a _____.
Then you will call upon me and come and _____ to me, and I will listen to you. You will
_____ me and find me when you seek me with _____ your heart."

Do you have the plans for your life?_____

Who does?_____

What is God's plan for us?_____

Here we see that word *hope* again. God wants to give us hope. Jeremiah was speaking to God's people, who were living in captivity. They were enslaved during the reign of Nebuchadnezzar and were held for seventy years in a distant pagan land. They were facing a difficult time as an ethnic group and as individuals. They were experiencing hopelessness, feelings of abandonment, an unsecure future, and captivity in a culture not their own, all while trying to maintain their identity and their families. Their life was bleak and looked depressing and yet God said He had plans for them. What they were experiencing right then was *not* their future. It was but a moment in their journey. They were in the midst of heavy struggles, and they couldn't see it but God had better things in store for them.

As a special needs parent, do you experience some of the feelings the Jews felt?_____
_____

Do you feel like you have lost your identity? _____
_____
_____

Knowing what the Jews had gone through before Jeremiah's message in verses 11–13 (abandoned, captive, hopeless), can you see how hopeful those words would have been to the people and how they relate to us today?_____

List the seven reasons for hope found in this passage of Jeremiah.
1)
2)
3)
4)
5)
6)
7)

As special need parents, we must put our faith in God's promises, trusting that He will change our lives for the better. God has a plan for even us. While the Jews experienced devastating trials and had no idea what their future would look like, God spoke through Jeremiah to give them hope. I can imagine that what God was telling them didn't make any sense because all they could see were their troubles. But God told His people to go on with their lives and to plan a future even in the midst of trials (vv. 4–7) because He would not forget them and would help them.

Our out of the ordinary special needs life screams at us to press on. While we face the bondage of being servants to our children with special needs, God tells us to make plans, to move forward, and not to sit back and let life pass us by. He tells us to hold on to Him because He will give us hope and our trials will turn into our testimony. Though we may be living in an unfamiliar land, navigating dark and dreary roads alone, with no idea what the future will be, God's plan is to prosper us, to see us grow and flourish right where we are. Each step forward, no matter how small, will bring us closer to Him. We can be confident that our present circumstances are for a purpose: to turn our story into His story.

Read Isaiah 26:3.

"You will keep in _____ those whose minds are steadfast, because they trust in you. Trust in the Lord God always, for the Lord God is the eternal rock."

We live in a world that will never be fully at peace. We won't see peace encompass all peoples; Jesus said as much. (See Matthew 24:6–7.) There will always be fighting, wars, and conflicts. But individually, despite our situations, and amid our own troubles, we can have peace deep down inside of us.

How does Isaiah say we can have perfect peace? _____

_____

What does it mean to be steadfast?_____

Why will we receive perfect peace if we have firmly fixed our minds on God?_____

_____

_____

Read Romans 15:13.

"May the God of hope fill you with all joy and _____ as you trust in him, so that you may overflow with hope by the power of the Holy Spirit."

Read John 14:27.

"Peace I leave with you; my peace I give you. I do not give to you as the world gives. Do not let your hearts be troubled and do not be afraid."

Jesus says He can give us peace that is not of this world; it looks nothing like what the world has to offer. His peace occurs when we are in relationship with Him. When we take the focus off of ourselves and widen our scope, we see that our circumstances are only part of a bigger picture. Our present circumstances are temporary, no matter how long-lasting they may seem. We will not face these challenges in our heavenly home. When we choose to have peace, not to worry or to be afraid, and find comfort in the peace Jesus offers us, He will help us be content no matter the trial.

Read Philippians 4:11.

"I am not saying this because I am in need, for I have learned to be _____ whatever the circumstances. I know what it is to be in need, and I know what it is to have plenty. I have learned the secret of being content in any and every situation, whether well fed or hungry, whether living in plenty or in want. I can do _____ this through _____ who gives me _____."

Here we find Paul giving us words of wisdom about how to live while he was enduring his own trials. He said we can find contentment despite our circumstances. We can have peace even though our situation seems bleak. We can choose joy. We can choose to be content. We can choose to trust. Even when we are facing another long day of taking care of the needs of another, we can draw strength from Christ and choose how we react. We can choose to have peace.

Do you think Paul always had an attitude of contentment?_____

_____

How did Paul's trials give him perspective? _____

_____

In what way have your trials given you a new perspective?_____

_____

Reads Proverbs 3:5–8.

"Trust in the Lord with all your heart and lean not on your own understanding; in all your ways acknowledge him, and he will make your paths straight. Do not be wise in your own eyes; fear the Lord and shun evil. This will bring health to your body and nourishment to your bones."

What six commands do you see in this passage?
1)
2)
3)
4)
5)
6)

We have a desire to understand why things are the way they are. Think of little children who ask why all the time. Their curiosity is insatiable; they always want to know why this and why that. Curiosity to figure out how things work drives people to become doctors, engineers, and scientists. It's the reason we ask God why when we don't understand. God created us with curiosity. But there will always be things that can't be explained, things that make us seek deeper answers with the hope that we'll find some profound understanding.

Proverbs contains warnings and practical wisdom for us today. We shouldn't depend on how we think things should be. We can attempt to achieve wisdom and seek understanding, but being wise in our own eyes is shortsighted and foolish. We need to lean on God for ultimate wisdom and truth, and when we do that He will make our paths straight. Or, as some Bible versions put it, "He will direct our path."

The rough patches we face on our special needs journey will be easier to navigate when we quit trying to do everything ourselves. Our walk will get easier when we stop relying on our own wisdom and seek God's wisdom. When we lean on Him, that bumpy path we're on gets smoother and easier to travel. And when our path is easier to travel, even our health will improve. Stress and anxiety can actually make us sick, manifesting themselves in physical problems that affect our strength, our walk, and even our appetite. And Proverbs tells us, with wisdom beyond the medical science of that time, that our health is restored to us when we fully lean on God and let His wisdom be our strength on our journey.

Let's read Psalm 23 with a bit of extra commentary to help us absorb what we've learned this week about hope, peace, and trust.

The Lord is my shepherd, I shall not be in want.
  God is like a good shepherd, providing everything His sheep need.
He makes me lie down in green pastures,
  The shepherd provides food.
He leads me beside quiet waters,
  The shepherd provides water.
He restores my soul.
  The shepherd provides rest for our spirits.
He guides me in paths of righteousness
  God leads us toward the right path.
For his name's sake.
  God displays His mercy and grace through us.

Even though I walk through the valley of the shadow of death,

   We will face darkness on our journey.

I will fear no evil,

   Even in the scary places, we needn't be afraid; God can be trusted.

For you are with me;

   God, our good shepherd, is always there.

Your rod and staff comfort me.

   The shepherd's staff guides us and protects us, leading us where we should go.

You prepare a table before me

   We are invited to the banquet to eat at His table.

In the presence of my enemies.

   God's bounty doesn't eliminate the problems in our lives.

You anoint my head with oil; my cup overflows.

   God refreshes us with His abundant blessings.

Surely goodness and love will follow me all the days of my life,

   We hope in God's care; it will be available to us throughout our lives.

And I will dwell in the house of the Lord forever.

   We will get to enjoy the presence of God forever.

Can you confidently say the Lord is your shepherd? _____

David's psalm reinforced what he learned over his life to be true: God is like a gentle, loving, and good shepherd. David was very familiar with the life of a shepherd, having been one in his youth. He knew how much care and devotion were required and how to faithfully provide for the sheep's needs. He knew how the shepherd guided the sheep and led them to eat and to drink, all while keeping watch for the enemy. The shepherd protected the sheep. We can compare our special needs journey to the journey of the traveler in David's psalm. We walk through dark valleys, we experience lows that cloud the sun, and we have the enemy waiting outside our door, but God is with us at all times. He always keeps watch over us and guides us to better places, allowing us to experience His goodness and His faithfulness on our journey. The valley may be taking us to greater heights if only we will trust the shepherd to lead us out. Greener pastures may be right beyond the dark valley. We need only to put our hope and trust in God, because He is the Good Shepherd.

Group questions

Have you had an experience like David's in which you walked through the dark valley and felt God guiding you? _____

_____

God does not promise He will remove our enemies or the dangers in our lives. How can you experience peace when your enemies are at the door?_____

_____

_____

Why do sheep represent believers so well? _____

_____

_____

Is it easier to praise God in your valleys or on your mountaintops? _____

_____

_____

Week 7 notes

_____

_____

_____

_____

_____

_____

_____

_____

_____

Jen's Journal
August 16
When Kyle Ann passed away, I began a journey that was undeniable life-altering. The path I had been walking had been abruptly closed off. I could no longer live my life and travel down the same road I had been going down. The path was blocked. I had to stumble about and find my way around the barrier in order to return to some semblance of my previous journey. I had become injured on the trail when I tried to go around as I stumbled about, but after struggling for a while, I found I had finally made it to a path that would take me where I wanted to go. The sun was shining and I was feeling good about my travels again. The path was a bit harder but still easy enough that I could look up to see in front of me.

I started to heal from my injuries and to see a bright future down the path. I could envision love, peace, and joy again. But then a storm arose, a tempest like no other, causing me to lose my view entirely. Brady and Liam were born way too soon. I couldn't see the path before me due to the storm. Darkness enveloped my trail. I couldn't see my way forward, and I couldn't see to go back. I became stuck.

Then the rain turned my dirt path to mud. As I stood there, unmoving, I became one with the mud. It enveloped me as an old friend and I sank deeper into its depths. And I allowed this to happen to me. I was not going to move from my path. The fear of the unknown and of the darkness around me kept me locked in place.

As I stood in my spot, unwilling to seek shelter or help, I was whipped and beaten by the debris from the storm. Not only was I frightened, but now I was also injured.

When the storm finally cleared and I could see the broken and damaged remains of my path, it became too much for me to comprehend. My journey was over. I couldn't go on. The road was no longer easy. The journey was no longer a walk. I would have to plod through thick disarray. How could I find my way through all of the mess? And how could I do that when I was so badly injured? How could I trudge on when I had so much muck to slog through?

I slowly began to move around and look for a way back, but I could see there was no way for me to go on. I could not do it alone. I cried out to God to show me the way and to help me get back to the trail I had been on. But He wouldn't show me that way again. He had covered over and hidden my old trail. He began to highlight a new path for me instead, one that was narrower than my previous one. The journey would not be easy, for this trail had twists and turns, with weeds and branches blocking the way. I knew it was going to be difficult, but I also knew this was the path the Lord had chosen for me. I could rest assured that this was the way that pleased Him, no matter how hard it would be for me.

I am still going down this difficult road. I am traveling ever so slowly because I still have hard work ahead. I am nowhere near the person I used to be when I was on the easy road. The harder road has shown me more things than I ever thought possible. I am still afraid, for I cannot see as clearly anymore what lies beyond the bend. I have had to put all of my trust in the One who does know.

I have experienced new sensations and thoughts that would never have occurred if not for the tempest. Why does pain have to be such an integral part of our humanness? Can compassion exist without suffering? Can bravery exist without danger? Can we experience pure joy without experiencing pain?

Before, I would never have even asked these questions, but now I can answer them.

Guide me in your truth and teach me, for you are God my savior, and my hope is in you all day long.

Psalm 25:5

Week 8

A New Normal

Grace means we don't need to airbrush our lives to make them look perfect when they're not.

—Bob Goff

Introduction

You have no idea how difficult circumstances can get until you have arrived at them. Then you think they couldn't possibly get any worse, but they do. That's the life of a special needs parent. It is such a roller coaster of emotions. While I was working on this chapter my own special needs son spent nearly a month sick with one fever after another. After a second round of antibiotics, he woke up with a fourth fever. Four different viruses/infections in a three-week time span that couldn't be explained. I thought we would be in the clear, so when the new fever popped up, I lost it. I burst into tears. I wept in the privacy of my bathroom and gave all my fears to God. But oh how I cried: tears of exhaustion, tears of frustrations, and tears of anxiety.

I am worn out. I haven't slept in a month, and I am emotionally spent. My son is inconsolable when he's feverish. I can't hold him. I can't cuddle him. He doesn't want to do anything. He doesn't want to be happy. And because I am his mom, not being able to help him makes me feel useless. It's my job to make my child feel better. I'm supposed to be able to help make things right for him. Do I just give up? Of course not. But the harsh reality crashing down around me reminds me that none of this is under my control anyway. I can never make everything right for him. His life will never be perfect; it won't even come close. His life is not under my control, only in my hands for a while, and we live a life of unknowns and surprises about what's coming around the next corner. The only thing I can know for sure is that God has us in His plan.

Special needs parents can spend a lot of time feeling like a failure. We can get beaten down and defeated. We are worn out, exhausted, and damaged. Life takes a hefty toll on us long before our peers with typically developing children. We get good at juggling and multitasking, but we spend a huge amount of time and energy on our children's needs, and the stress of parenting can undermine our long-term health. We can experience negative consequences from our special needs journey. We face burnout, exhaustion, depression, and anxiety. Some parents experience physical problems helping their children deal with mobility issues which can create joint pain and back problems. And some parents suffer from anxiety-based post-traumatic stress disorder, or PTSD. Throw in our relationships with our other children and our spouse, which still needs our attention, and you have one bone-weary and drained parent. No, our special needs journey is not for the faint of heart; we often have to fight to rise out of the trenches.

Yet some of our most vital growth takes place down in the dark places. As strange as this may sound, we have some things in common with the potato. A potato has everything it needs inside of itself to grow. You can hide a potato away, preventing light from getting to it, but while down in the dark, it will attempt to grow and develop new shoots. It seeks to grow despite its circumstances. It makes use of its environment no matter where it lies. The darkness cannot hinder the potato's growth. Like the potato, God has already equipped us with what we need to grow. Even in the darkest of times, there is a divine element inside of us helping to grow and develop us, to push us out of the darkness and into the light.

We don't have to have it all put together to be used by God for His purposes and His glory. He grows us while we are still in the dark, making use of us no matter where we lie.

Lord, this week help us to learn how to better manage our new normal. Teach us how we can move from simply coping to truly thriving. Show us in Your Word the wisdom we need to endure the trials we will face, and help us not to become worn out when we feel like we are stuck in the dark.

"Commit to the Lord, whatever you do, and he will establish your plans" (Prov. 16:3).

Read Galatians 6:9.
"Let us not become weary in doing _____, for at the proper time we will reap a harvest if we do not give up."

Since the daily grind of our special needs life can be so draining, sometimes making it hard to do good, we have a unique twofold perspective of this verse. We can read it from a Christian perspective and from a special needs parent perspective.

Every one of us grows weary and burned out. Have you ever joined a gym with the intention of sticking to a new exercise routine only to fail to follow through with working out? What about the enthusiasm you initially had for teaching at your church? Has your excitement about serving waned as you realize it just isn't as much fun anymore? Have you excitedly rejoiced at finding a new therapy or routine for your child only to discover it is difficult to stick to the changes the therapist recommends? New opportunities get us excited, but when the thrill and excitement fades, it's relatively easy to give up and quit, to grow tired of doing good. Following through can be difficult, especially if we are on our own or have no support.

What does Paul mean when he says not to become weary in doing good? _____
_____
_____

Paul had just been telling Christians in Galatia the things they needed to avoid and how to live their life worthy of the Christian calling when he offered this encouragement to do good. In Galatians 5:19–21 Paul talked about the evil things we should shun. Then he immediately followed that up by naming the fruits of the Spirit, the good traits we will exhibit when we follow the teachings of the Holy Spirit.

Read Galatians 5:22
What are the fruits of the Spirit? _____
_____

Which fruits of the Spirit are your strongest?_____
_____

Which do you feel you lack the most?_____
_____

Have the fruits of the Spirit been strengthened in you since you had your child with special needs? Which ones?_____
_____

When we have the fruits of the Spirit dominating our lives and our attitudes we will do the good Paul speaks about. We can often get tired of doing good when we don't see results. As Christians, we grow weary of praying for someone who doesn't want to change, of circumstances we face that never get easier, of doing good in the face of evil and never feeling like we are making a difference.

Our special needs journey presents the same problem. We pray for healing for our kids and we don't receive it; we work with them on their special needs and we don't see any positive results; we get worn out from trying to do all the right things when we don't see any good occurring from our efforts.

Have skills or therapies you've diligently worked on with your child born no results that you can see? _____

_____

Have you experienced burnout from the tasks required of you each day in your journey? _____

_____

How can you regain your enthusiasm to better care for your child? _____

_____

Paul knew we'd grow tired. His encouragement in verse 6:9 is there to remind us that we won't always see results right away, that we may not even see results until the end and sometimes not at all. Some of us will even get results we aren't expecting. But Paul says that at the proper time, we will reap the harvest from the seeds we have planted. We will eventually receive our reward from the giver of life and all good things, for all the good we do, but we might not get to see any of the rewards in this life. We do not labor and do good things for our benefit, to give ourselves a pat on the back. We labor for the Lord and for His purposes in our lives, that He may be glorified through us.

Read 1 Corinthians 15:58.
"Always give yourselves fully to the work of the Lord, because you know that your _____ in the _____ is not in vain."

Special needs parents can experience the same criticisms a Christian faces. We will encounter ridicule, harsh opinions, confusion, judgmental ideas, disparaging remarks, lack of support from family and friends, even persecution for holding a belief about our children that doesn't fit with mainstream societal views.

Unfortunately we will most likely have to deal with difficult people and situations. In fact, it's highly probable we won't escape our special needs journey unscathed by the ignorance of others. It's how we handle ourselves in these circumstances that will show others where our joy and hope truly lie.

One morning when my son was very young, I took him to the park for a ride on the swing. He has no head control and needs full support to swing. He was not quite big enough for the special needs swing but little enough to still hold in my lap. Two girls about eight or nine sat down in the seats beside me; one of them sat on the special needs swing. A girl about seventeen years old started pushing her in it and said, "You are such a retard! You're sitting in the retard swing!" I drew a sharp intake of air in shock. The little girl laughed, echoing her by repeating her words. The third girl, on the regular swing, started in as well. "You are so retarded you have to sit in the retard swing." The two young girls ridiculed "retards," all the while laughing at their jokes while using the swing for physically handicapped children. I wanted to throw up.

I was deeply hurt and so mad I was shaking. I knew I couldn't say anything rational while that angry, so I didn't speak up at first. The girls conversation shifted to discussing their IQs and who had done better on their end-of-the-year tests. One of the girls said her score was better, so she obviously was not the "retard" in the group. As I held my little boy, who would use a special needs swing, who couldn't defend himself against such ignorant and painful words, I decided I needed to say something. I wanted them to know there are real people and families affected by their off-hand remarks.

I prayed for wisdom, strength, and the appropriate words. I hoped this would be a teachable moment for them and for me. I turned to the girls and said, "You really shouldn't use the word *retard* because it's not nice. That is not a retard swing. You are sitting in a swing that is meant for people with disabilities. Having a physical disability or any disability at all does not make someone retarded. Actually, *retard* is an old medical term that simply means slow, and it is offensive to use anymore. Doctors don't even use it." They just stared at me.

That was all I felt I could say. I don't know if they understood what I said or if they even cared, but I knew I had to speak up and try to teach them how wrong they were to use such a hurtful, demeaning word. I tried to layer my speech in love, knowing their ignorance of the word did not necessarily reflect who they were inside. I had been a frequent user of the "r-word" in my younger years, before my son came along. I didn't understand the full impact of using that word around people who face disabilities and the prejudices people have against them. But I do now, and my hope was that they would too.

We will face situations in our lives in which we can lash out in anger at the ignorance we encounter or we can turn it into a teachable moment.

Does a friend question your child's diagnosis?
Do your in-laws disapprove of your child's therapies?
Has someone said you just need to pray away their disease or diagnosis?
Has someone told you, "You just need to pray harder."?
Has a stranger told you how you should parent your child?

Have you had someone diagnose your special needs child?
And my favorite question: "What's wrong with him?"

We need to ask God to help us grow in our trust of Him despite our circumstances so we can help reach and teach others in the process. My son is just as valuable and worthy of bearing the image of our Creator as those girls in the park are. There is nothing wrong with him. He is exactly how God intended him to be. That's what we want the world to know. Our children are important, valuable, and worthy. God made them unique on purpose, with lives full of meaning. The good we continue to do, despite our circumstances, will be an example to others. We will bear the fruit of love and joy in our attitudes and ultimately in our hearts, and it will branch out, reaching others.

Have you ever experienced criticism from a stranger about your child?_____

_____

How did you react?_____

_____

The Holy Spirit gives us the power to do what is too hard for us to do with our own abilities. Instead of becoming angry and shouting at people who don't understand, we can ask God to give us peace in our hearts and love for others so our words will be gentle and kind. I am in no way saying this will be easy to do when opinionated people misplace their thoughts and speak them out loud in our hearing. I've had the, "What's wrong with him?" question in the middle of a McDonald's and trust me, I fought my desire to be snarky, and went with what I knew God wanted me to say. We can be momma bears, naturally defending the honor of our kids and fighting to protect them. But we can also choose to be gentle, giving soft answers as we teach others about what they don't understand. God is willing to help us. We need only ask for His help as we teach others how we want our kids to be treated. They will learn from our example. They will look to us to guide them on how to engage with and treat our children.

Read Philippians 4:6–8.

"Do not be anxious about anything, but in everything by _____ and _____ with _____ let your requests be made known to God. And the _____ of God, which surpasses all understanding, will guard your hearts and your minds in Christ Jesus. Finally, brothers, whatever is true, whatever is honorable, whatever is just, whatever is pure, whatever is lovely, whatever is commendable, if there is any excellence, if there is anything worthy of praise, _____ about these things."

Paul told the persecuted believers not to be anxious. The people were literally losing their lives for their faith, something that still happens around the world today. Avoiding anxiety is a hard thing to do on our own but not impossible when we seek God and His will for us. We can do what needs to get done. We can do one more therapy; we can make it through one more outburst and one more IEP meeting; we can love on one more person who makes an ignorant comment, because we do it with Christ, who strengthens us. We are to focus on what is honorable, what is pure, what is lovely, and what is commendable: the fruits of the Spirit.

Write Philippians 4:13. _____

_____

We cannot do these things on our own. We aren't meant to and Paul knew it. He knew without a doubt that God gives us the strength to endure. God gives us the strength to make it one more day when we don't think we have the energy to go on. Remember, Paul wrote from his experiences. He endured much while bound in faith to Christ, and he knew God would give us the strength and wisdom we need if only we ask Him. Special needs parents are not exempt from trials, and neither are Christians. Life will drag us down and get difficult, but we have a beautiful hope over those who do not know Christ. During difficult circumstances our hearts, minds, and attitudes must remain rooted in the One we know will help us to weather the storms.

Can you do everything God has called you to do? No, not in your own strength. But you can when you allow Jesus Christ to be your strength.

Read Psalm 28:7.
"The Lord is my _____ and my shield; my heart _____ in him, and he _____ me. My heart leaps for joy, and with my song I praise him."

Read James 1:2–4.
"Consider it _____ _____ my brothers whenever you face trials of many kinds. Because you know that the testing of your _____ develops _____. Perseverance must finish its work so that you may be _____ and _____, not lacking anything."

James, Jesus's brother, wrote a letter to Jewish Christians to encourage them when they faced trials. He didn't say *if* they faced trials; he said *when*. He knew no one is exempt from facing trials that will test their faith.

Our faith in Christ gives us strength not only to endure during the tough times but to grow in maturity and wisdom through them. Our contentment in Christ helps us run to the only thing that truly matters when circumstances are difficult and out of our control: God's kingdom.

As we go through trials we can choose to act as if God is good and actively involved in our situation, or we can choose to act as if He doesn't hear us, doesn't care about us, and is unable to bring anything good out of our struggles. James reminds the followers of Christ that we can trust our trials, that they have purpose. They will add up to joy when we count on God through them. Our confidence in our perfect Father will be strengthened, and God will bring us to perfect completion through them; we will lack nothing in our characters.

Have you faced a situation that wasn't initially positive but turned into something beneficial and God-honoring? _____

_____

_____

Read James 1:5–8.

"If any of you lacks _____ he should ask God, who gives _____ to all without finding fault, and it will be given to him. But when he asks, he must believe and not doubt, because he who doubts is like a wave of the sea, blown and tossed by the wind. That man should not think he will receive anything from the Lord; he is a double minded man, unstable in all he does."

How does James say we are to ask for wisdom? _____

_____

How does God provide this wisdom? _____

_____

James concludes his statement about trials with an insightful point; we might be facing our trials without seeking wisdom from God to help us through. We need wisdom and guidance from the Lord to help us navigate our troubles. James tells us not to doubt or to be double-minded in our asking. We aren't supposed to let ourselves get tossed around. But what exactly does it mean not to doubt? Does it mean that if we have any doubts at all, God won't hear us? What if we are only 75 percent positive God will do what we ask? What if it's 90 percent? What if we are 99 percent sure? Does this tiny bit of doubt mean God won't let us receive what we've asked of Him?

God works with doubters all the time. Remember Gideon? He doubted. So did Sarah, Moses, and Thomas, and the list goes on! The Bible is full of doubters, people who questioned because they lacked confidence and because they didn't understand. But James applies an additional adjective to doubters: they are unstable. They haven't put their roots deep into the ground to grow strong and be fruitful. They become uprooted when the strong storm comes. As James illustrates, they are tossed around by the waves and can't stand firm in their faith. Allow me just one more illustration. Doubters are not like the faithful sheep, who follow their shepherd on the safe path; they fall off course and get lost along the way.

Read Proverbs 4:25-27

Let your eyes look _____ ahead, fix your gaze _____ before you. Make level paths for your feet and take only ways that are firm. Do not _____ to the right or the left; keep your foot from evil.

When I was learning to drive, I swerved all over the place and couldn't keep the car evenly between the lines. A friend told me I was fixating on the spot right in front of the car and that was making the car swerve erratically, jerking it back and forth in the wind. He told me to look out farther down the road to where I wanted the car to go. I needed to keep my eyes on the horizon. The horizon would be constant and unchanged in front of me, and that would keep my gaze fixed and steady. Once I did that, I was able to keep the car securely in my lane and I couldn't be knocked off course.

Our special needs journey is kind of like learning to drive a car. We are not to fixate on the very next step on the path but to look up toward the finish, even if that finish is simply collapsing into bed at the end of another exhausting day. If we hold our gaze steady toward the horizon, keep our focus, and seek wisdom from God, He will guide us to our destination. Yes, sometimes all we can do is take one more step. And that single step is a victory all on its own that should absolutely be celebrated. But we can get stuck in the muck if we hold on to doubt and don't trust the way.

Read Job 12:12.

Is not _____ found among the aged? Does not long life bring _____?

Read Proverbs 12:15.

The way of a _____ is right in his own eyes, but a _____ listens to advice.

Read Proverbs 15:12.

"Mockers _____ corrections so they _____ the wise."

Read Proverbs 15:22.

"Plans fail for lack of _____, but with many advisers they succeed."

Is there anyone from whom you should not seek advice?_____

_____

Have you ever received advice about your child that was poorly given? _____

_____

We will often be forced to make a major decision, determining what we think the best course of action for our children should be. We will need to seek advice from wise people and sometimes from multiple sources in order to make the right choice. We want the best for our children, and seeking advice from foolish sources won't benefit our kids in any way. It might even harm them. The same goes for us as followers of Christ. If we seek advice from the wrong sources, we are not partnering with God in our actions or decisions. We can set ourselves up to fail when we remove God as our guide and listen to insincere or irresponsible counsel.

Read 1 Thessalonians 5:16–18.

"Be _____ always, _____ continually, give_____ in _____ circumstances for this is God's will for you in Christ Jesus."

What is God's will for you? _____

_____

Notice the adverbs *always* and *continually*. These words describe a constant state of being, no matter our circumstances, and not something that is done just once in a while. We are to be active participants in our walk with God. We are to be joyful, praying continually, and giving thanks at all times. Praying continually is probably the easiest of the three. Finding joy and giving thanks in all circumstances might be a bit more challenging. In fact, it is utterly impossible to do if we depend on our own abilities in our daily struggles. Only with God's help can we accomplish this. God wants us to change our attitudes and shift our focus on His will for us.

Read Psalm 32:8–10.

"I will _____ you and _____ you in the way you should go; I will _____ you and watch over you. Do not be like the horse or mule which have no understanding but must be controlled by bit and bridle or they will not come to you. Many are the woes of the wicked but the Lord's _____surrounds the man who _____ in him."

What will God do for us? _____

_____

Sometimes our prayers seem to go unanswered, and we aren't sure which direction to take. At times we cry out for advice and we don't get a solid yes or no response. When we are unsure, what do we do then?

Read John 14:16–17.

"And I will ask the Father, and he will give you another _____ to be with you forever—the Spirit of Truth. The world cannot accept him, because it neither sees him nor knows him. But you know him for he lives _____ you and will be _____ you."

Notice the word used is *Counselor.* Our Father has given us a helper or advocate known as the Counselor. It's a legal term for someone who helps those in trouble. That's the radical love our Father has for us. He has given us a counselor to turn to, a helper the world doesn't have, when we are in trouble. The Holy Spirit is working within us, and we can seek His wisdom at any time, asking Him to help us and to advocate for us.

We are instructed to seek wisdom, to pursue godly counsel, to study God's Word, and even to fast for an answer to our prayers. But what if we still aren't sure what we are supposed to do?

Read 1 John 5:14–15.

"This is the _____ we have in approaching God: that if we ask anything according to _____, he hears us. And if we know that he hears us—whatever we ask—we know that we have what we asked of him."

Whose will do we seek? _____

When we approach God with our requests, seeking His will for us, what do we receive? _____

_____

What can we know for sure? _____

We are assured that God hears our prayers. They do not fall on deaf ears. However, our will doesn't always line up with God's at first, which is why we might not be getting the answer we seek. But the more we grow in our faith and humble ourselves before the Lord, leaning toward His will, the more our prayers will align with God's desire for our lives and the more we can be sure of the answers we seek.

Read Psalm 55:22.

"Cast your _____ on the Lord, and he will _____ you; he will never let the righteous fall."

Read Psalm 46:1–3.

"God is our _____ and _____, an ever-present help in trouble. Therefore we will not _____, though the earth give way and the mountains fall into the heart of the sea, though its waters roar and foam and the mountains quake with their surging."

Are you feeling weary and worn out? Do you seek wisdom and still feel unsure? Do the demands of parenting your child with special needs leave you feeling exhausted and spent? Do you wonder how you can make it even one more day? Do you feel all alone?

Read Matthew 11:28–30.

"Come to me all you who are _____ and _____ and I will give you rest. Take my yoke upon you and learn from me, for I am gentle and humble in heart, and you will find _____ for your souls. For my yoke is easy and my burden is light."

What is a yoke? _____

_____

Why would Jesus compare our burdens to a yoke? _____

_____

Jesus's followers would have understood this analogy quite clearly. A pair of draft animals would be harnessed together with a wooden beam consisting of two U-shaped pieces that hold the animals steady and allows them to work as a team. They are no longer two animals trying to do their own thing but one team united and bound together to meet the same goal.

This invitation from Jesus beautifully illustrates how to work in tandem with Him, allowing Him to guide us and to carry some of our burdens. Jesus is telling us not to shoulder the brunt of our burdens alone but to call on Him to help carry our load. When we are yoked with the One who is able to help us bear our problems and trials, we can carry on with our burdens without being fully weighed down by them.

Do you ever feel defeated and overburdened by your situation?_____

_____

Have you accused God of not caring about the weight you carry? _____
_____

Does this illustration by Jesus help you to better bear the burdens you've been carrying?_____
_____
_____

Our sweet children are missionaries in their own way. They really are. While they may not be able to go into all the world and preach the gospel, they are teachers in their own right. They are little warriors fighting for the truth that they are loved and valued by our Creator. They show not only us but those around us what it means to trust fully in the One who created us all. They unknowingly evangelize everyone they come in contact with and in turn teach us how to tell others about the great news of Jesus. While my son has never purposely been a missionary, God used his life and his story to call me to Belarus to work with families and their children with special needs. My testimony about God and His goodness and faithfulness in the midst of broken dreams and a diverted journey has brought Liam's story halfway around the world. My nonverbal son reveals the mercy and grace of God more effectively than I could ever testify to on my own.

God is creating a beautiful story out of your journey. You are impacting others. It's your experiences, your testimony, and your triumphs that reveal God's story in your story. It may not look that way right now. Your situation may seem like a big, ugly mess. Your struggles may feel pointless. You may feel like your life is never going to look normal or even come close to having it all together. But that's okay because it's not supposed to. That's the beauty of God's amazing grace. He meets us right where we are down in our messes and in our beautiful brokenness and tells us He doesn't want us to look like everyone else. He wants you to embrace your new normal. He's chosen for us to be different. We don't need to seek society's version of perfection because society has it all wrong. God has a much better plan. None of us has it all together, and you don't need to because His grace is enough. You don't need to know the ending when you trust the Good Shepherd is guiding you every step of the way.

Group questions

Our unique special needs journey gives us the opportunity to see beauty where others can't. How can you share the truths you've learned? _____
_____
_____

Have you felt the Lord strengthening you on your journey so far? _____

_____

_____

Are you willing to let God use your journey, your grief, and the healing you've found to teach others about how good He is? _____

_____

_____

While your journey is far from what you might have had in mind for your life, can you rest securely in the knowledge that it is the one you are supposed to be on? _____

_____

Week eight notes

_____

_____

_____

_____

_____

_____

_____

_____

_____

_____

Jen's Journal
February 16

I used to interact regularly with a large number of social groups—friends, homeschool groups, church groups, work groups, parents of my kids' friends. But after having Liam, my involvement in these groups has either fallen to a bare minimum or has ended entirely. People have disappeared from my life. Friends I used to have dinner with are gone. It's unfortunate to lose such important, supportive friendships. My social interaction is now with therapists, teachers, and Facebook. And the social circles of which I was once a part are now foreign to me.

I have had to reconcile myself to the fact that this life is not my own. I always knew it wasn't. But acknowledging that is very hard to do when you have the illusion of control for so many years and then realize you never had it to begin with. But I haven't done this grudgingly. On the contrary, while

I very much miss the life I used to have—the freedoms, the money, the friends—I have found joy in places that most people will never know: watching my multiply disabled son smile when I enter the room (even though he doesn't really see), celebrating every little step forward he takes (each one a giant leap for him), and seeing the love his brother and sisters share with him. He delights in their attention, and their view of people with disabilities has broadened their hearts and minds.

Our new normal has not been easy. It's not been easy at all. I struggle with how best to be a light in a dark world when I feel like my own world is very dark. My faith is in a transition phase, and I have learned that even though I may walk away from God, He has not walked away from me. I am at a crossroads where I do not know how to be the best me I can be. My old self is so familiar and the skin I wore so comfortable. I have been put in a place where I do not know the new me very well at all. On any given day my emotions run full tilt in opposing directions. I face situations that I don't want to be in. I imagine that is a lot like how Moses felt. He was put in a position that he did not feel comfortable with and did not feel capable of handling. He argued with God about whether He had picked the right person for the job. I most certainly feel the same way. I ask myself every day whether I am the right one for this job. And day after day I wonder how my light will shine when my social system has been destroyed. I am unable to go into all the world. I barely get into the world at all.

Why put me in a position where I have no certain impact beyond my family?

The Internet has surely helped lessen the isolation families like mine experience. I am saddened when I think of all the families that struggled before the dawn of texting, e-mail, Facebook, and Google. Even in my isolation, I know I have it better than those families. I can reach out online to other moms who have children with special needs, and not just children with CP. I can relate to all such moms because I can empathize with them. Every parent experiences the same range of emotions—anger, denial, frustration, grief.

I remind myself that my job is not to worry about where I go, whom I see, or who sees me. My job is not to worry about money or about my needs and my wants. My job is to trust that I am where I am supposed to be and that God will use me if and when He sees fit. How can I be a light when I am stuck at home? How can I go into the world and show the gospel? I don't know yet. But I do know that through Liam's journey I have met more people online than I ever thought possible. God has taken us to physical and emotional places I never would have gone without having a special needs child. Although my social circles have shrunk to a bare minimum, who knows how and in what way God will use our story?

Commit to the Lord whatever you do, and your plans will succeed.

Proverbs 16:3

A Final Look

Now that we've wrapped up the last week of our study, let's take a quick look back at what we have learned through this journey together.

1) We are chosen by God to raise and care for children with special needs. Some of us were called in advance to the title of special needs parent, while some of us had the position thrust upon us unexpectedly. In either case, God knows you and your child and loves you both fiercely. Your journey is not hidden from His view. He sees you and cares for you even when you may not feel like it. Your story matters.

2) God is sovereign. He has full control over even the minor details and orchestrates things to work out even when we can't see how this could possibly be. His providence can be seen when we look back at situations and see His guiding hand at work. Our lives as special needs parents has not taken Him by surprise.

3) Grieving over the life you thought you would have, or the life you did have, is to be expected. Your life has taken a turn you didn't see coming. Adapting to the changes in your family life, your friends, and your finances will take time. You will need a chance to process and to grieve, and that looks different for everyone. Don't be too hard on yourself or on others as you learn to navigate the bends in the road.

4) God adores people with disabilities! He does not view them as less than anyone else. We need to realize that the brokenness fully seen in those with disabilities points to our own inner brokenness. We are all broken and in need of Jesus Christ. God's compassion and tender care for those who feel less than others remind us that He views us as all the same.

5) We are all *imago Dei*. Regardless of ability or disability, class, ethnicity, or gender, we share the imprint of God. We are unique, valuable, and worthy of love because our Creator put something of Himself in each one of us.

6) As followers of Jesus Christ we are called to service. Jesus was the ultimate example of how to live life serving others. When we serve the needs of our families and of our special needs children, we point others toward Jesus. He is the reason we can have hope on dark days. When we serve others, we serve Christ.

7) When we fully trust God and allow Him to be our shepherd, guiding us on our new journey, we will gain confidence and peace that the path we are on is the right one. Though things won't make sense and the road will get tough, He will gently guide us along the way. He won't abandon us in the dark valley.

8) We can find joy in our new normal. God wants us to plant our roots deep in His Word, to trust Him, and to grow in our faith. We are not alone on the journey. God wants us to lean on Him when our burdens are too heavy and to let Him help carry the load. He is our strength, and when we rely on Him, He makes us stronger and helps make our struggles worthwhile.

Afterword

Never be afraid to trust an unknown future to a known God.

—Corrie ten Boom

I want you all to know how grateful I am that you have made it through this study! God placed this study on my heart four years ago, but I shelved it when I got halfway done. And there it sat while life moved on. I developed health problems, and my son got older and harder to care for, but my trust in God continued to grow. After I got my health problems under control, I felt the pull to start again where I left off in this study. I talked to a friend and asked her to keep me accountable. I told her to make sure I worked on the study each month. I said that if the only thing that ever came of the project was to say I'd finished it, so be it. I would be happy. God would do something with it if He wanted.

I never intended to write a chapter on the providence and sovereignty of God, but I knew He was calling me to do it. I was scared about writing that chapter, and as I finished it, I decided to see if any companies would be interested in publishing my book. Seriously, the providence of God is incredible, and I soon learned why He had me write that chapter. The first woman I spoke with at the first company I called, out of all the people working for all the publishing companies, was able to relate to my story. You see, after the stillbirth of my daughter, Kyle Ann, I had my twins prematurely, causing Liam's issues. This woman was born prematurely after her stillbirth sister, and she faced some special needs because of this. That is not a coincidence, my dear friends! That is our Father, making Himself known on the question of whether I should publish this study. By putting this woman in my path God lovingly arrested my fears.

This study was written just for you. God cares for you. He loves you so very much, and He wants you to know you can trust Him on your journey. You never have to travel down the dark road alone. He appointed you to care for and to raise a child who has special needs. He invites you and your sweet family to enter, disabilities and all, and to eat at His banquet.

Please feel free to reach out to me at anytime! I'd love to meet you, hear how things are going, offer words of encouragement, or just pray with you. You can always find me on Instagram at jenmcintosh_ or on Facebook at www.facebook.com/clearlyirish or feel free to drop me a line at www.justblog.me.

How to Start a Support Group

Do you feel called to lead a support group? Connecting with others facing the daunting task of parenting special needs kids is vital. The love and support you provide to other special needs parents might be the lifeline they need to help them thrive. If you don't have a support group in your community and would like to start one but don't know where to begin, here are a few tips to help you get started.

1) Pray. Ask God for direction. Ask Him to lead you on how best to care for and to support your local special needs families.

2) Figure out where to meet, how often, and at what time.

3) Talk to your pastor. There may be members of your church who would love to get together, and your pastor might be willing to let you meet at the church.

4) Determine how much time you have to devote to the group. Consider finding a partner who can help you when you've had a tough week.

5) Decide whether you are going to provide child care. Most single moms won't be able to meet during the day due to work. If you meet in the evenings, these moms will need someone to watch their kids so they can come. I recommend not meeting with the children present so you can be more open and share your needs without interference from the children and without their little ears hearing too much. Provide child care if at all possible.

6) Talk to the moms you know who have children with special needs. Honestly, it doesn't matter if the needs are small or severe. You'd be surprised at how many moms just want to interact with another mom who gets what it's like to be floundering around in life and missing normalcy.

7) Talk to your children's doctors and therapists. They have a connection to parents that others don't, and they can help you spread the word that a support group exists.

8) Put up fliers. You can put them up all over, from coffee shops to therapy offices. No one will know your group exists if you don't get the word out.

9) Remember that the group doesn't require a structured program or Bible study. Many parents will not have a chance to do a study or it won't fit into their schedules. It's okay to meet just to fellowship with each other, to drink coffee, to share prayer requests, and to lend an ear. Parents don't need anything fancy, just the opportunity to talk openly and to know they aren't alone in their journey.

To be honest, I never had any desire to start a support group. I have felt like Moses more times than I can count, convinced I am not able to speak before people. And yet, through a series of conversations and circumstances, God propelled me to the position of a special needs parent support group leader. When I first started the group, there were only two of us (Thank you for sticking with me, April!). We met every other week for months. I felt awkward leading this "group" and didn't understand its purpose. In the years that followed, God led both men and women into our group, allowing us the privilege to get to know them and their special children. We have spent many a time in prayer and thanksgiving for the smallest of gains and have cried over each other's struggles. We have used Bible studies and have also spent time just talking about our problems. Our members and their needs have morphed and changed over the years, but one thing has remained the same: we can all come to each other for prayer, no matter the need, knowing we aren't alone.

It's okay to feel inadequate to lead a group. God loves to amaze us and to use the least expected. I promise you God will give you what you need if you only ask Him. He will use your devotion to Him to develop in you the confidence and the competence to accomplish what He's called you to do.

"Find rest, O my soul, in God alone; my hope comes from him" (Ps 62:7).

Notes

Week 2

Donald McKim, *John Calvin: A Companion to His Life and Theology.* (Oregon: Cascade Books, 2015)

Week 3

Elisabeth Kübler-Ross, *On Death and Dying* (New York: Scribner, 1997).

Week 4

Americans with Disabilities Act. US Statutes at Large 104.327–78 (1990).

Merriam-Webster.com., s.v. "disabled," accessed April 3, 2017, https://www.merriam-webster.com/dictionary/disabled.

Merriam-Webster.com, s.v. "broken," accessed April 3, 2017, https://www.merriam-webster.com/dictionary/broken.

Week 5

R. A. Webb, *The Theology of Infant Salvation* (Harrisonburg: Sprinkle, 1981), 288–89.

Printed in the United States
By Bookmasters